SCHIPPERTAINMENT

SCHIPPERTAINMENT
LIFE AS A SCHIPPERKE OWNER

WRITTEN BY RICHARD DAVIS
ILLUSTRATED BY AMY CURRAN

Dedication

This book is dedicated to my mom, Niki, and my Schipperke family. My love has no depth when it comes to my Little Black Devils. Love and licks from the Idaho Pack.

SCHIPPERTAINMENT: LIFE AS A SCHIPPERKE OWNER

Copyright © 2018 by Richard Davis.

All rights reserved. No part of this book may be used or reproduced in any manner whatsoever without written permission from Pink Coffee Publishing or Richard Davis.

Published by Pink Coffee Creative
PO Box 483, Oberon NSW 2787, Australia
www.pinkcoffeepublishing.com

Written by Richard Davis
Illustrated by Amy Curran
www.amycurranillustrator.com

Book Layout and Cover design by Amy Curran

ISBN: 978-0-6482393-5-2

10 9 8 7 6 5 4 3 2 1

CONTENTS

FROM THE AUTHOR	7
TRIBUTE "NIKI"	9
WE ALL GET THE FLU	13
SCHIPPERIDING	21
A FUR KID FROM HEAVEN	33
LIFE HISTORY OF A GIVING SOUL	40
GAME ON	47
A LITTLE PERSONAL ABOUT ME	53
IT'S TIME FOR A TRIP	59
SCHIPPERLAB	67
NEVER TRUST A DELIVERY GUY	78
SCHIPPERVIZING THE REMODEL	83
THINGS THAT HAPPEN AT CAMP STAY AT ...	90
WALKING THE OWNER	100
SHE JUST RAN OUT THE DOOR ...	109

FROM THE AUTHOR

I am a simple old guy in the mid-sized town of Boise, Idaho. I have made it through fifty-nine years and hope the good lord gives me a few more. I've been a car wash kid, a burger flipper, a welder, and a veteran. I am proud of my service with the Air Force and I served with distinction. I did four years' active duty and in that time carried my duffel bag and toolbox around the world. And then I served in the Air Guard for two years, fulfilling my military obligation. But my heart is and always will be with my brothers in arms. Regardless of the branch, they go into conflict each and every day to protect my right and your right to do what we want to do. As Toby Keith said, "I'm an American Soldier, an American. Beside my brothers and my sisters, I will proudly take a stand."

Take the time to consider to the words. My book will be sold worldwide. To Schipperke and dog lovers worldwide, and we will continue to protect worldwide. My hope is that this book will bypass the barriers of politics. Of language and colors. Of race and religion. And give each of you a chance to just forget what's going on in the world for a few minutes. A few hours. A relief. A breath of fresh air.

Share with me the love, the hilarity, and sometimes, the sorrow. This is not just about my fur kids. This is about me and my life. My love and prayers go to all that take that time to sit and enjoy. Contemplate about life, as I have. And buy more little black devils.

TRIBUTE

4/4/10 to 1/15/18

Novelist Erica Jong said that "dogs come into our lives to teach us love, and they depart to teach us loss". As Schip-parents I think we can all agree that this is true. But I think they all teach us more than that in their own special and unique way. I know mine have. But this isn't about my dogs, although I could certainly fill pages with anecdotes about their antics and what they've taught me. This is about Niki.

Most of us know Niki's story. She was born with hemi vertebrae, a condition that eventually left her back legs paralyzed. She had a host of other medical issues that left her human mom with no choice but to say goodbye. She was just shy of her 8th birthday. We mourn her loss and know she is running free forever over the rainbow bridge. She has lots of company with which to get into Schipper-mischief.

She was a Facebook celebrity. We avidly followed her mom Arlien's posts, eagerly waiting to see what this Schipperstar was up to, hiding under the bed, getting out of her wheelchair, scooting around, loudly demanding her dinner. All of Niki's antics were adorable because they were her antics. Through social media, her funny, spunky, quirky, and determined personality jumped right off of the web and made us smile. Her joie de vivre was obvious, even on her hardest days. We should all be so lucky.

Niki taught us to live life to its fullest, no matter what fate throws our way.

Heaven is a little bit brighter now that she is there – for I believe that all dogs go to heaven. Know this – if we had a Schipperke walk of fame, Niki would have a huge and shiny star. Rest in peace, little one. Run free. You taught us all so much.

– Melissa Lamont-Gordon

This tribute was written by Melissa Lamont-Gordon (Melissa Lynne), on behalf of the Facebook group Crafty Schipperke People, of which Niki's mom is a member.

WE ALL GET THE FLU

As we all know, dogs have a tendency to remain close to us regardless of the circumstances and situations. The only exception is when you attempt to give them a bath. My Luci and Coach are retired show dogs and they both figure that they have had their lifetime quota of baths on the circuit. Therefore, it's somewhat difficult to get them to stay in the vicinity of the bathtub when I am attempting to give them a little clean-up.

Now, I'm not a mean daddy. I don't just throw them in there with vim and vigor and water them down. Nope. I carefully lay a towel in the bottom of the tub so that they don't get those uneasy shaky legs so apparent in dogs. Then I warm the water up to the precise temperature that will calm and sooth their tired, overworked bodies. I have this oatmeal shampoo with oatmeal conditioner that helps their coats glisten in the sun and in the living room lights. Then I go out and get the dogs.

Coach first, because he's the baby about this cleaning up thing. Ok, now the game begins. How is it that I can take a million showers and have constant companions leaning in trying to grab my wash towel or razor? They organize a coordinated attack. One comes from the front and one from the back. I hear the shower curtains rustle. The attack has begun.

Coach is the distraction this time. He's scratching on the back of the tub to confuse me. My hand goes out to pet him but away he goes in a flash of skittering paws on the bathroom floor. He disappears. I turn around to grab for the washcloth that moments ago was placed over the handle. I suddenly realize something. It's winter. Not summer, where we would enjoy the cool feel of a cold shower. No way. It's 22 degrees outside. And my washcloth's gone. And the dogs are gone. And the water temperature has gone from a warm, pleasant 120 degrees to the arctic blast of 50 degrees of full-on cold water.

Now, I cuss sometimes. I cuss when I stub my toe. I cuss when the Idaho traffic slows to a snail's pace for a combine. I cuss when my dogs get loose. And I cuss when Luci grabs my washcloth and turns the water to full cold. Ok, back to the bath. Where are the dogs?

I have only had Coach and Luci for about a year. And I have not been completely trained yet. I still have willpower and the strength to handle the Schipperhypnotism. That moment when you know the dogs are going to do something, but you can't stop it. They look at you and it's melt time. Ok, go ahead. Do it. I'll deal with the aftermath.

I can't seem to find them in the usual places. On the sofa sleeping? Nope. Looking out the front window, proudly protecting our little plot of soil from transgressors such as UPS and FedEx drivers. And an occasional mailman. Oh, and the neighbor kids taking their daily walk around the neighborhood. That has them tearing up the blinds, trying to show their disapproval of them just walking by. But they're not there.

Out in the backyard? No. Ok, I'm getting nervous. I run and check the gates. Locks intact. Dog poo on shoe. Fence is intact.

Under the deck? No way. I started by putting 1 by 4 cedar fence pieces under the deck to prevent them from journeying under there. I ended up with 2 by 4 interlinked and dug down to China to prevent them from going under. I walk quickly around the deck and can't see any weaknesses to my fortress. Another dog poo-covered foot. I'm about to dial 911 and say my babies have been kidnapped. I pull the poo-laden shoes off at the back door and run inside in a panic.

As I round the corner, about to grab the phone, I see a paw. Just a hint of one hanging out of the carrier. We all know that Schipperkes that are on the show circuit spend most of their time hanging out in their personal condo. A little plastic box that has a smelly but familiar blanket and some water. That's a place of comfort for a show dog. Their pad. Their place. Where they can just lay back and relax. Chill.

Now, I don't know if they watched me as I ran around in a panic, but I bet they did. The last place I would look for them is in the kennel. And that's where they are. The shower has been running for twenty minutes and the hot water is going away. So, they get a delay in their sentencing. As I cook dinner, I notice smiles on the faces of my two pups.

That evening, I start to have chills. It's winter so I crank up the heat a little. At 65 degrees, I relent and crank up my trusty pellet stove. It uses mini presto logs on an auger system to feed the fire. Once you get it started, it takes care of itself for days. The temperature in the house goes up into the 70s. I have a blanket on my lap and a heating pad on my back. Yea, I'm getting old, but am in denial.

Soon the dogs are panting. I'm thinking that maybe I stressed them out trying to give them a bath. Snack time. They crawl up on each side of me and start to snore. I'm happy, but man, I'm still cold. I rearrange the canine heating blankets as I settle down on the sofa to watch some Star Trek and Gold Rush reruns. The dogs snuggle up knowing that they have missed the bath bullet today. Tomorrow. Lol.

Now the temperature's in the high 70s and for some reason my canine heating blankets are not regulating my temperature into the comfort zone. Suddenly, they start to pant. Great. Now what? Not one, but both. And they move over by the front windows. I crank the heating pad to nuclear, and crank the pellet stove to the sun setting. I have surpassed my thermostat's ability to keep up with the temperatures and the dogs are rolling around in the snow in the backyard. Guess it's better than rolling in the mud pit I had last year.

They are standing outside as to mock me. We are nice and warm out here in the 20s and you are freezing your butt off in the 80s. OMG. I'm sick. Grab the cold and flu arsenal from the bathroom cabinet. Whew. I have this covered. The dogs are laying in the snow on the back patio. I'm worried they might get too cold, so snack time. You see the clever ploy they are introducing into my plight. I grab them a snack and me a bottle of NyQuil. I was a fireman for years and an Emergency Medical Technician (EMT). My mom was a registered nurse all her life. I know how to shake off this minor glitch in my immune system. I have this covered. I'm not sick very much.

I needed intervention this evening though. My body ached. Not just a little pain in the hands and arms. My body hurt. My whole body. From my toenails to the hairs on my head. I hurt. I'm miserable. And the dogs are sweating. I can see that from my sofa covered with two blankets and a comforter. And a nuclear heating pad. As I was ready to guzzle a bottle of NyQuil, I thought to myself, I wonder what the expiration date is?

Just checking. What? Not 2014. No way. Ok. Breathe deep. You have an unopened bottle right there. I grab it and, just for the heck of it, check the date. OMG, 2012.

The dogs are rolling around in the snow. And I swear they are laughing. My caring, loving, and affectionate Schipperkes are laughing at me. I'm annoyed. Breathe deep. You have this under control. We all know that when you get sick, your temperature goes up. Einstein moment. I'll get in the shower and warm up. Maybe that will break my fever. Regardless, it's got to be warmer in there than here on the sofa. The dogs are looking at me with curious expressions as I head out of their view and into the bathroom.

Now, we know that dogs are smarter than humans. Most of us choose not to accept that fact. I am a believer. They foiled an attempt that very morning to get baths. But my concern wasn't for them as much as it was for me and some warmth. I start the shower. The towel is still in there from my earlier failed attempt at dog washing. I grab a blanket for my head and after adjusting the temperature to just shy of scalding, in my skivvies, I hop in and lay down.

The memories of my college life flash before me. My memories of being so drunk that the only safe sleeping place was the bathtub. It tremendously reduced the next day clean-ups. I have grown up since and have no use for the tub. Although the toilet has been an option a few times after weddings. Oh well. So, I'm lying there adjusting the temperature with my foot when I hear a scratch on the side of the tub. I had closed the curtain because it being open created an uncomfortable draft. But I open it a little just in case. As I'm lying there, I look up and see Coach leaning over the edge of the tub with his head stuck inside, checking me out. I reach up and touch his head and he leans in to get a wet hand scratch on his head. He backs out and I lie back down.

As I'm lying there, counting down the minutes to an empty hot water heater, I just sort of go into a nice, comfortable bliss. My blanket has my head supported and the towel is cushioning my hips. I am warm and life is good. The curtain moves and Luci pushes it aside. I open it up and Coach is right there. When I open it, Luci full on jumps onto the blanket that is supporting my head. Coach isn't far behind. I curl up a little and they both lie down, in the shower, with the water running and snuggled with me till the hot water runs out. I crawl out and dry both them and me off, then head to the bedroom. It is cold in there but they both lie next to me. I feel warm even as I freeze with that fever. They don't leave my side all night.

We, as humans, think animals are below us. That they don't have the brains to understand things that we understand. That they can't understand pain and feelings as we humans do. I know my fur kids feel and love. When they do something wrong they know to beg for forgiveness. They know that they can always lie next to me and get belly rubs. They know I love them with unconditional love and that I will protect them to my last breath. They are my fur babies, but I still can't get them into the shower.

My next clever ploy is to buy an oversized kitchen sink. With the addition of a new tankless water heater, I have unlimited hot water now. So, I can wait. I will stalk them. I will lull them into a false sense of security. And I figure, at least the first few times, that I can blind side them while they are looking for tidbits on the floor. Hope springs eternal that they will eventually either get too old to avoid me or just give in and accept their destiny.

I pray daily. And the shower awaits.

SCHIPPERIDING

We all have taken our fur kids on rides. And we all live with the consequences of doing so. Some are good. Others are less than good. I have seen the good and the bad on my side.

My wife, at the time, and I, bought a 28-foot camper trailer to tow behind our full-size Blazer. When we first hooked it up, I asked myself why did I need a 28-foot trailer for two people and two dogs? A Coleman Pop Up would have done just fine. Much easier to maintain and so much easier to drag around civilization. But no, she wanted room for friends and family, and the neighbors, and the homeless. You get my point.

I was towing the Queen Mary around 360 days a year just for that one special weekend getaway with everyone else. And I had to get a special weight transfer hitch to keep the front tires on the ground. All for that one weekend each year, when we tow 100 miles, at five miles to the gallon, at 35mph, to roll into a campground with hot running water and bathrooms. Talk about roughing it. I had to use my own bathroom just so I could rationalize draining the sewage tanks. Everyone else thought that was so uncivilized. They kept saying, "Just go use the lighted bathrooms a quarter of a mile away." My reply would be, "Listen, I bought this trailer so we can rough it out in the boonies. And I'm going to fake it that I'm out in the boonies, no matter what you guys say."

So, I backed the Queen Mary into a spot just a little bigger than a postage stamp and hooked up the water and the sewage. Women pressure. They all stared at me till I relented and plugged the trailer into the power. Then they all ran in there and cranked both A/C units to the max. All the while, us guys were outside swatting flies and donating blood to the mosquitoes. Did I fail to mention that we have mosquitoes that are on par, size-wise, with hummingbirds? The women were inside the trailer drinking like fish and playing Canasta. I'd never heard of the game. But we anticipated strip poker before the night was out. All us guys were high fiving each other. But, little did we know that the trailer was taken over. For the weekend. By the women. For their personal and private use. They even moved the beer and hot dogs into a cooler, placed it outside the trailer, just for us to use. Inside, they were cooking steaks in the oven and mixing foo foo drinks in the blender. They were laughing and giggling like little kids. Till around twelve midnight.

Now, I never figured out the witching hour, till this weekend. Us guys had pretty much finished the barley pops in the cooler. And my resentment about hot dogs instead of steak was down to a more tolerable level. Heck, they didn't even throw out any condiments. And used sticks to cook them, on the fire we had to start with matches. Matches we pilfered from the neighbors. It wasn't settling well with us. The siege was on. They were going to recover their spouses and I was going to have a good night's sleep on my queen-sized bed with cotton sheets and a down comforter. I was happy in the thought. Till I walked in the trailer and saw the carnage.

There were cards, all over the place. There were drinks, all over the place. There was uneaten steak, all over the place. Three days of me and steak dinners had been wiped off the face of the earth. In one night. By a bunch of women on a food binge. There were open boxes of munchies all over. It looked more like the aftermath of a hemp party, than a card party. But, in their defense, they cleaned up the areas they were sleeping in. Eight women, in my camper, in varied states of sleep, snoring almost in unison. It was a moment in time where you have to think out things very carefully. This could explode in our faces and make for a really bad weekend. Another two days with women, who we had just woken up. Better judgment prevailed. We retreated and analyzed the situation. After further study, we pulled out the sleeping bags and headed to the leftover accommodations. I burned up that night in my sleeping bag. I was two layers away from the guy I was sleeping with in a two-man tent. But I still slept with one eye open.

The next morning, we were all awoken by gentle hugs and kisses from our other halves. They had coffee, bacon, eggs, toast, and hash-browns. I had sleep deprivation. But, all us guys high fived each other behind the trailer. The weekend was a success. I pulled the trailer back down the mountain to our humble abode. It took two days to clean up the mess from that one night. I found snacks in places you shouldn't have food in. I had to take my trailer sewage system to be unplugged professionally because of something they put in the toilet. I gladly paid 200 dollars when they started mentioning what they managed to flush out of it. But it was a success. People think it's so cool to have the freedom to just be able to pull over when you want to and check out the world. I agree. To a point. We took a weekend trip to a little-known place called Warren, Idaho. Feel free to pause here and Google Maps the community.

It's a long way from everywhere in the middle of Idaho. We decided we would pull the trailer up there and stay just outside of town by the dredge ponds. They stock these ponds with trout and it's easy to catch your breakfast, lunch, and dinner with just a cast and a worm. The road is all paved till about thirty miles out of Warren. Then it's a zigzag dirt road that is a little wider than a driveway. We were towing the Queen Mary. Each meeting with another vehicle was a challenge. We went into the barrow pit and they avoided sideswiping us. It was mutually assured destruction. The road hadn't been worked on for a couple of weeks and had some washboards. Those in the know are aware that washboards have a certain rhythm to them. And if you don't follow that rhythm, your teeth and equipment are subject to damage. We followed the rules as best as we could and found a spot just outside of town. I unhooked so we could go into town and get dinner.

There was no need to lock the doors out there. There was nobody out there. It was starting to get dark. We got to the bar/store/eatery/post office/meeting place and parked. Right next to the horse. As we walked in, we were greeted with silence. Everyone, all eight of them, turned around and stared. At that moment, I had to pull out my trump card. I said, "I'm a veteran and the next round is on me." I developed a great friendship with eight people that night. We watered up the cook and received massive ribeye steaks cooked to perfection on the barby in the back.

After what seemed like hours, we made it back to our camper. It was darker than the Ace of Spades out there. We had parked in an area with tailings from the long ago gold rush. After we both got our rock legs, we made it in the camper. The inside of the trailer looked like Sasquatch had gone through it. The mirror was on the floor. The dishes were all over the floor. And my Cap'n Crunch was all over the floor. I was upset about the Cap'n Crunch.

We cleaned up a little and decided to relax outside and enjoy the view. The mosquitoes were not bad, so we got out and shut off all the lights. Sitting in chairs, we looked up. The sky was crystal clear and you could see forever. No light pollution, no clouds, and no smoke from fires. The Milky Way was spread before our eyes. It was so beautiful. After a while, we retired to the queen-sized bed I had seen so few times. As we laid down, the sound of the world came into our camper.

A camper isn't like a house. Exterior walls with two by fours and insulation. Interior walls with paint. Nope. It's aluminum foil exterior with quarter-inch foam. There's nothing there if you need protection. From bears and wolves, to Sasquatch. Just saying. Now, we had batteries on our trailer. And propane. We could start a fire and light you up. Well. I left the interior lights on when we left and the batteries were dead. My bad. No big deal. I had a generator and we could recharge in the morning. And propane would warm us up, when I got the generator running in the morning. As we were lying there, we heard a sound of someone or something coming towards us. You could hear the rocks moving around outside. It came up to the trailer and was sniffing around. I could hear the breathing. I was wide awake and on point. She was asleep and snoring. Why didn't I bring a gun this time? I thought to myself, imagining the headlines. Trailer gets trashed by   ? I thought a frying pan would help, but really? It was big. It leaned up against the trailer and scratched it. I was thinking Godzilla had escaped and come to Idaho. Ok.

If I'm going to the pearly gates tonight, I want to see what is taking me. I looked out the window. Nothing. I go to the door. Look out. Nothing. Really. Ok. I'm going to open the door. If there's something out there, my girly screams will surely alert the other half. Then she's on her own. I'm surely going to get sucked out into the netherworld by the critter outside. I hear another noise outside. The cooler is getting beat up on. Come on. Don't take breakfast and lunch. And dinner for tomorrow. Ok, rethink this. Take it all. Then you won't be interested in us. I look out the door window and see the cooler disappear around the back. I head to the bedroom and grab the blinds and yank on the cord. She wakes up. Is anything wrong, she asks. I didn't want her to know she was about to be eaten, so I said nothing. As I looked out the window, there I saw it. As my cooler was dragged across the rocks, I saw. This little black bear that couldn't have been more than 100 pounds, dragging my full cooler into the brush. It was almost comical. He had hit the jackpot. And he was dragging this huge Coleman cooler full of goodies into the brush. I locked the door.

The next morning, we went and got breakfast in Warren and I told my story. As the locals rolled on the floor laughing, one of them said it happens to everyone. I recovered what was left of the cooler about 100 yards from the trailer. It was trashed, but I wasn't about to leave it out there. I don't litter. It did take me a few hours to clean up the paper and wrappings. I figured he or she was lying up in the forest, bloated, laughing at me.

We pulled out the next day, filled from breakfast and much wiser from our experience. Everything was on the floor or bed to prevent breakage. We got home and I was over this. I wanted a motorhome. And more protection. My other half said we needed to try just one more time. Ok.

This time we take the dogs. Sasha and Gizmo were my first Schipperkes. Gizmo was my 'puppy mill' Schip from Emmett, and Sasha was my first purebred Schipperke. We decided to take them on a trip to Stanley, Idaho. The trip is a windy road but we had taken the kids on day trips before. Surely they would be ok. I loaded us up and headed into the mountains of Central Idaho. We had gone about thirty miles and decided to stop to give the kids a walk. We wandered around the trees for a half hour, then loaded up. On the road again. Gizmo was asleep on the back seat but Sasha was insistent on being on my other half's lap. We pulled a blanket out and Sasha sat on her lap as we progressed towards Stanley.

Now, we have all seen that look on a Schipperke's face. It's that look that says, "I'm so over this." Followed by the total and complete contents of their stomach and intestines being sent in every direction. The blanket helped. I laid on the brakes and came to a stop in front of this beautiful house and property. My trailer and Blazer blocked the drive, but I had priorities. Get all of that out of the Blazer. When I hit the brakes, Gizmo thought it was time to get out. He jumped from the back to the front and landed in the contents. But he was so happy. I jumped out and grabbed him. Sasha was on the floor. The blanket was soaked. I got a leash on him. Then Sasha came to me. Gizmo was in the other half's control and the blanket was on the ground. Everyone smelled bad. My brain kicked into gear. I had an outside shower. Wahoo. I took Gizmo over and cleaned his paws and chest off. Hand off. I took Sasha and washed her up. We had to use baby shampoo on her, because she was just a mess. As I was washing her down, she looked up at me as if to say, "Daddy, I'm sorry."

I couldn't be mad at her. It was my fault for dragging them into the mountains on these zigzag roads. I got her cleaned up and we broke up a Dramamine and gave half of one to each of them. After a half hour, we proceeded up the road with an abbreviated trip. We got into Lowman and turned onto Bear Valley Road. As we wound up the canyon, it started getting dark. Our weekend trip was cut down to surviving the night and return trip. We found an opening that we could just fit into.

Up here, if you can find someplace to park on the roadside, you can do it. There was a running creek 10 feet away and pine trees all around. I leashed the dogs up and we went for a forever walk. The fur kids were in heaven. The new smells and sounds were just overwhelming for them. They were pulling right and left. Forward and back. They had to check out everything. Every tree was new. Every bush was new. Every turn was a new experience. We walked for a couple of hours. When I got back, dinner was served to me and them. As we sat by the creek, they were still just taking in the sounds and environment. It made me wish I hadn't taken so long to give them this experience. I took them to the creek to drink and they just stood in the cold waters, licking up the cold, clean water. The night came to an end and we crawled into the bed. Sasha laid down. Gizmo got on the bed and promptly let me know he didn't appreciate the ride by peeing on the comforter. But, I couldn't be mad.

Schipperkes have their own special way of letting us know they are unhappy. Gizmo's way was to do that. I heard the flood start and rolled over. In one perfect motion, I rolled him gently onto the floor and curled the comforter into the corner. We always carried extra linen, after the girls' night out. So, I just took the comforter out, laid it in the stream for a few minutes, then hung it in the trees. I went back in and pulled round two out and laid it down. Sasha and Gizmo laid down and we all slept.

The next morning, as we loaded up, I realized my pups didn't appreciate the trips as much as the new smells and environments. So, we continued walking them all around the valley till they went across Rainbow Bridge in 2016.

Boise is an amazing place, with many diverse environments. We have a beautiful river running through the middle of town. On both sides is public space we call the 'Greenbelt'. This runs for miles in both directions from the city core. We also have many miles of hiking trails into our foothills and throughout our community for walking, running, and biking. It's our little secret. Don't let others know.

My new fur kids, Coach and Luci, have had a sniff of Boise. Next summer, they will be ambassadors for the Schipperke family. The two pictures you see in this story are of my gone, but never forgotten, fur kids. Sasha is the first picture and Gizmo is the second picture. In their memory, I dedicate this book to them and Niki.

Dogs are brought into our lives to teach us many lessons. The joy of a new meeting every time you walk in the door. The short time they are on this earth with us teaches us to live each day as if it is our last. And the deep pain as they finish up their journey on earth as our heart children and ask us to do the final act of love. To release them from the pain their bodies have endured in those short years being at your side. And hold their heads up, with tears in your eyes, as they cross onto the Rainbow Bridge. You are the last loving look they give and receive as their spirit leaves Earth.

Most of us choose our faith. Most of those that read this book believe in spiritual presence. We all have had moments that we feel the spirit of our kids across the bridge nudging our leg or breathing on our neck as we lie in bed. They are our little spirit angels, guiding new fur kids into our lives to reduce the pain and heartache of our losses.

Schipperkes are hard to get one's hands on. And when you do, it's because you were sent that fur kid from your little angels. Care for and love them with passion. Treat their ills and revel in their intelligence. They will challenge you mentally and physically. They will give you love unlike any other pet has ever given you. They will be mischievous, and stubborn.

But please never raise a hand in anger to a Schipperke. Once that bond is broken, you can never get it back. Train them and stand watching with pride as they overwhelm you with their agility, speed, and presence. They are a proud breed. A noble breed.

They are Schipperkes.

A FUR KID FROM HEAVEN

I automatically assume that everyone that reads these stories are Schipperke owners. And if you have other breeds, I thank you for giving those amazing pups a forever home. I have owned Schipperkes for two generations. That is, I have lost two, to old age, and I'm on my second generation. I have to say that my life hasn't been full of gold, glitter, and accolades. But I'm still here on Mother Earth, so I must have another purpose. I'm a giver.

Each year, I take the tickets I have from my social visits to the local Dave & Buster's and purchase stuffed animals. During the Christmas holidays, I spread these stuffed animals around the valley. St Luke's Children's Hospital, the Meridian Police Department, the Boise Police Department, the Ada County Sheriff, and the Idaho State Police. This year, I chose to deliver over 400 stuffed animals to the 'Christmas at the Depot' sponsored by Boise Parks and Recreation. This is my way of helping others.

When I got my second round of Schipperkes, I introduced them to my friends. One of them fell in love with them. Tammy would ask me to come over a few times a week to let the dogs run on her huge landscaped property. It gave the fur kids a chance to spread their legs, because my yard is rather small. It takes yards to get a Schipperke up to zoomies speed. Not feet. They would run with wild abandon and run over each other with excitement. Tammy swears it was to get me over there, but I think it was for the dogs. She absolutely fell in love with these two little black dogs.

I was casually thumbing through Facebook and happened to see a somewhat disturbing post. It said, "Purebred Schipperke pup. Must find new home ASAP." The pup was in Coeur d'Alene, Idaho. That's 380 miles or seven hours of driving from here in Boise. I had been looking for a Schipperke for Tammy and, as we all know, it's next to impossible to get one. But the stars must have aligned that day. I called and left a message, trying not to be pushy. Ten minutes later, I decided what the heck. Get pushy. I left another message saying I was headed that way in the morning and would see them around 3:30 p.m. No response. Take a chance and drive 800 miles just to not get him. Oh well. The things one does for those he cares for. I rented a Nissan and at 'oh dark thirty in the a.m.' I headed up north. When I got about halfway, I called again and someone answered. I breathed a tentative sigh of relief as she said the pup was still available and she would ask the owner to hold it for me. Now, pedal to the metal in the Idaho backcountry will get you in trouble with critters such as deer, elk, cows, and the occasional local yokel police officer. So, I minded my manners and did just a little under warp speed up north, keeping a vigilant eye out for the Mounties.

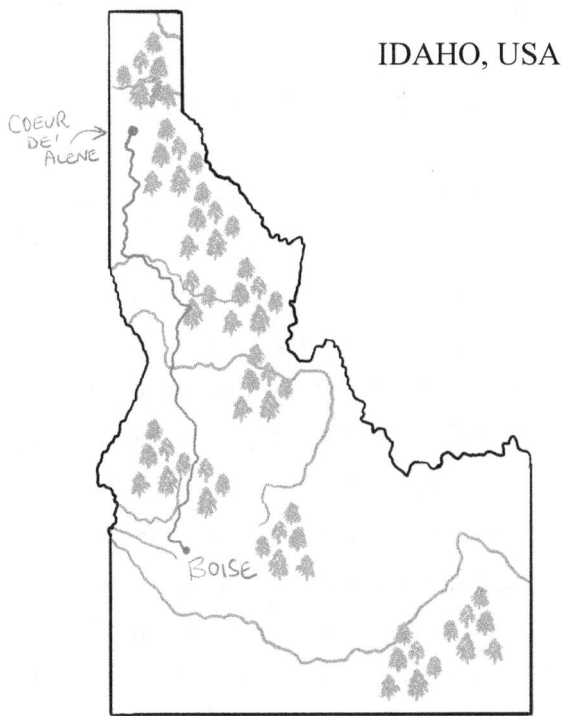

As I pulled into Coeur d'Alene, I stopped and called the breeder that was arranging this marriage. She said this: "The dog is at another person's house because it bit the first owner. And the caretaker is not off work till 5 p.m." There is not much to do in that two-horse town, in the afternoon, on a weekday.

So, I went to the breeders to do paperwork and get documentation on the mom and dad of this little hellion. She said the pup was sold to a mom that had an autistic child. And this 17-year-old had a severe form of it. Asperger's syndrome. Her mom bought this pup because the pup was so cute. And she thought that it would be a good companion for her daughter. I don't think there was much effort made to research the breed. Just confirmation that it was cute. Here's where I got on my podium of a soapbox and informed everyone in earshot that it is irresponsible of a breeder to sell a dog to someone that clearly has no idea what they have got themselves into. Schipperkes are an amazing breed. They are very intelligent and stubborn. And they react when you hit them, with these things called teeth. When I met the mom and daughter, so she could say goodbye, she was distant and really didn't know what was going on. Finally, the woman showed up with the pup. She said his name was Bear and it was perfect for this dog. He had bitten her and attacked her boyfriend's pants, leaving holes and an upset boyfriend. They all seemed relieved to get rid of this problem child. I must admit, I had some reservations when I heard all the horror stories about this mean, vicious, untrainable, biting dog. But I had faith. I had to think there was a reason this had happened. For all those stars to have aligned. For me to be there in that moment, rescuing that pup. The girl attempted to hug Bear, but there just wasn't any love there. He growled at her and growled as they put him in the cage. He was underweight, dirty, and smelly. I put him in the back, just to get him away from the environment he was in, and headed down the road. When I got to the other side of town, I stopped to give him some water and a walk. As I opened up the cage, he leaned towards the back and looked at me. This pup had had a rough start. He didn't deserve the hand he was dealt, but I was determined to make it up to him. I sat there, for what must have been hours, but was probably ten minutes. I just let him do what he wanted to do. He gradually came forward. I put my arm in the cage and he sniffed it. Then he went back into the back of the cage. There I sat. I took my jacket off and bared my arm and put it back in. He came forward and sniffed it. His tail wagged. Yes, Bear has a tail. An amazing Schipperke tail. A tail. I loved it. He let me put a leash on him and I carefully lifted him out. He was very tentative about moving, but as we walked, he started to get a little more excited. I stopped and leaned down. He came up and put his nose on my hand. I touched his chin, but he moved away. No bites so far. What is it about this pup that makes him so mean? I thought. He hasn't been mean to me yet.

We loaded up and headed down the road. I got a burger and gave him a little piece of Dramamine because the roads were pretty zigzaggy. I just tried to make him comfortable. We got to Lewiston and stopped at the top of the hill, to look over the Lewiston valley. He came up to me and let me put the leash on him. I gently lifted him down and he just stood there and breathed. In and out. In and out. He smelt the smell of freedom. I knelt down and he came up and nuzzled my arm and leg. I put down the back seat and moved him forward from the economy section. By the time I got to the bottom of Lewiston grade, he was talking to me. We have all done it. You stick your hand into the back seat and let your pups know you are there. To comfort them. But my arm was getting sore trying to lean back and drive too. So, we stopped again. And he moved to the first-class section. As we drove, we started to talk. He started with a little growl to get my attention. Then he started talking when I said he was going to his new forever home. And this conversation was amazing. Each time I spoke to him, I received a reply with a gentle growl or a snort. Schipperkes sneeze as a gesture. Or they have lint in their noses. I must admit, most of my time was spent with my hand in the cage, just touching him.

We made it to New Meadows and I was worn out. I got a room and took the cage and him inside. I got the food out and some water. We took a lot of walks that night. At 1:30 a.m. But, it was his time. His choice on what he wanted to do. He ate, he drank, he ran around for thirty minutes dragging me behind. Then we got back to the room. I had no clothes but what I was wearing, so I left the cage open and laid down for a few hours' sleep before the final drive home. As I rolled over, I felt a whisper. A warm breath. And a wet nose. Bear had jumped up on the bed. As I laid there, he crawled up on my pillow and started the Schipperke prep for sleep routine. Scratch, turn. Scratch, turn. Then he laid down. He was dirty and smelled like he needed a bath. But he laid down, in a little ball, on my pillow, in my bed, and snored. And we slept. The next morning, he was a different dog. His tail held high, and we cruised the trees with authority. With dignity. He rode with me to his new forever home on my lap. Curled up in a little ball with that tail wrapped around him. On my lap. I was smiling. I rolled into Tammy's and my two pups were there.

There was some concern about Bear interacting with the two older dogs, but all turned out well. Luci gave him an attitude adjustment and told him who was boss. He understood. Coach showed no interest in tangling with him, so life was good. Tammy hasn't been speechless many times since I met her. But this day, she was beside herself. Her baby Bear had arrived to his forever home and everyone was happy.

LIFE HISTORY OF A GIVING SOUL

I remember my first day at the Dave & Buster's here in little old Boise. That was five years ago. I also remember how excited I was when we got a mall. No. Not a strip mall. A real drive to, get out of your car, walk a mile in the summer heat mall. We have Sears, Macy's, and Victoria's Secret. That day, I realized we had become a big city. More than the capital of Idaho.

In this mall, opened Dave & Buster's. It was an experiment for them to build a property that was smaller to accommodate the smaller markets. I had heard that it was like a big kid's amusement arcade. And I missed those days of Donkey Kong and Space Invaders. To top it off, it offered a bar and food. I was in heaven. When I walked through the doors, I froze. I was immediately taken aback by the game sounds and bright lights. The staff and I got along well, so I decided to try some games. At first, I was just enjoying the tickets coming out when I won. But then I started to win a lot of tickets. A lot. Tens of thousands. Every time I went there. I cashed them in for various stuffed animals to give to random kids and saved the rest on my card. And so it began. Throughout the year I would play games and save those tickets. For what? No idea.

One night I was playing the game above. It's called Ice Age. I saw this beautiful little girl, who could barely walk, just sit down in the tickets and start playing. Her parents were taking pictures left and right. All of a sudden, she stood up and grabbed an armful and off she went on a high-speed walk towards the 'Rewards Zone'. This little girl had just started walking. And already she was shopping. She strung tickets from the front to the back of the store. And I stood there and watched her parents taking pictures left and right. I broke off the end of the string and told her parents to gather up those tickets and buy her something in the 'Rewards Zone'. I was a rock star. A hero for the night. My heart warmed up. My sad past was melting away.

It was late November, when the Toys for Tots brought in boxes to Dave & Buster's so that patrons could fill the boxes with things they had won. These toys and stuffed animals went to the children, of the Treasure Valley, that would otherwise not have a Christmas. I had an overabundance of tickets, so I filled a box. Literally, I filled a box. The management came by and thanked me. The Marines thanked me. My heart was filling up. That first year was the start of what has become an annual event for me. I play games all year in anticipation of buying stuffed animals to donate to charities and hospitals. I have donated to St Luke's Children's Hospital, Boise Police, Meridian Police, Idaho State Police, Ada County Sheriff's, and St Al's Hospital to mention a few. Each year for the last five years has gotten bigger. The snowball effect. Now, let me tell all that I just didn't walk in and throw a

few quarters down and win a load of tickets. I had to play games. I learned to play the hard way. Remember how hard it was to do the first level of Super Mario? Well, this is new technology. They have multiple ways to extract your money from you. They can adjust speeds of features. They can adjust delays in the response to inputs. They can randomize the features to make it impossible to predict how the game will react. Yes, I learned with my wallet. But

I learned. And I continue to enjoy the challenge of beating them at their game. Last year I surpassed 200 stuffed animals. And delivered them all over the valley.

But this year I have had a rough year. I lost my mom at 90 years young. She flew on the wings of angels and left this world. Her body is now free of pain and her mind clear again. I knew this was going to be a lonely Thanksgiving and Christmas, so I needed to make something special happen. I had hundreds of thousands of tickets on my card and thousands of game chips, so I started my vigil. I came a few times a week and played the games I could win at most. My total count was over half a million tickets to buy stuffed animals. The staff and management of Boise Dave & Buster's were amazing. It took a couple of weeks and a lot of double-bagging. I ended up with sixteen full 55-gallon bags of stuffed animals. Now what? An activity to deliver them to.

Boise Parks and Recreation was having Christmas at the Depot and I contacted them about my plight. Although somewhat skeptical about the numbers, they said I could arrive at 6:30 and the Marines would receive the toys. They had no idea what they were getting into. I was ready to put the shock into some kids and parents. I contacted my dear friend Don Rowling for use of his utility trailer. He said sure, come on over and I'll help you. He had no idea what he had just gotten himself into. I did. I bought a plastic Christmas tree, garland, and lights, and headed over to Don's place. He had put the trailer in the garage, so I started carrying in bags of stuffed animals. He watched the first load come in. Then the second. Then when I turned around to head back out he asked if there were any more? Only thirteen more bags. He froze. You know when your hard drive freezes up? It just locks everything up. That was Don.

We brought everything in and I started to build up the tree and decorate it. I got it decorated and the lights on it. Don was taking pictures of the pile of stuffed animals and mumbling something about this being over the top. I smiled. My elf's hard drive unfroze. We proceeded to wire the trailer for power and lights. I started tearing the bags of stuffed animals open and stuffing them into the trailer. Bag after bag. At halfway I started stuffing them in the tree branches. Needed room. We filled the front up to the top of the side rails. And back towards the rear I went. Stacking layer after layer. We opened the last bag, tossed them in, and closed the back gate. Lights, check. Tree, check. Stuffed animals, CHECK. I hooked up and off we went to the Depot. We drove right up to Capital Boulevard, which is the main entrance to the downtown core. People were honking, taking pictures, and some were giving me something like thumbs up. I wasn't driving very fast because I didn't want to blow over the Christmas tree.

We pulled up the hill into the Depot and came to a stop. Out came the coordinator and the look on her face was one for the record books. Shocked puts it mildly. She asked me if I wanted to come in and say hi to the kids. "Really, this isn't about me. This is about the kids," I said. She gently took my arm and guided me into the Depot. I thanked the kids and families for participating and said I needed help unloading a trailer of toys from Santa. Those kids lined up and helped the somewhat overwhelmed Marines load all those stuffed animals onto the Marine sled.

As we finished up, the coordinator came over and asked me to give an interview for them to post on their Facebook. In the interview, I held steadfast. "This isn't about me. It's about the kids of Treasure Valley that will wake up with something to hold and cuddle that they never would have gotten but for an old guy with a heart that was filled this last Christmas."

GAME ON

All of the seasoned, well-trained owners know to never run after your Schipperkes if they happen to loose from their leashes or leads. Schipperkes, as we know, put their heads down and run at warp speed in very random directions. Every smell's a new adventure. Every corner's a new smell.

Needless to say, unless you are a track athlete with major speed, you stand no chance of catching an on-point Schipperke. Those that have retired show dogs have a better chance of calling them back. An exception being me. Now, I have come up with a call for the dogs. I have practiced it a million times. It involves treats and, yes, it's bribery. Yet, the only words that seem to come out of my mouth in moments of panic are of the four-letter nature. A cog in my mind slips gently over to mouth in overdrive. And my mind races to keep up. Of course, the mind fails miserably, resulting in this gibberish that flows out of my mouth that only the cavemen would understand. And nuns would get their crosses out for. The result often is me on the pews on Sunday saying quietly to myself, "Bless me Father, for I have sinned."

Schipperkes bring the best and the worst in owners. Our undying love and willingness to overlook transgressions is the best. Our worst can vary in severity and sometimes be downright foolish. Mine seem to constantly border on the foolish. You would think that after owning Schipperkes for two generations, that I would have learned. The keys. You come in the house after a hot day driving truck. The dogs are basking in the AC flowing out of the ductwork at a pleasant 60 degrees. Outside it's over 100 degrees. But the fur kids are comfortable. That's all that matters.

They reluctantly jump up from their blissful sleep to greet you with excitement, licks, and patty cakes. As you close the door, the cool flush of air hits you. You lose all mind control. You have been Schippertyzed. That's when a Schipperke distracts you from your primary goal and gets you to focus solely and completely on them. There is no one else. Nothing else matters. Just them and them alone. You talk in an infantile voice and say silly things that we, as Schipperke owners, choose not to divulge. And after a few minutes of Schipperlove, you head towards the most comfortable place in the house, other than on top of the AC ducts. The shower. That fortress of solitude that once you enter, no one can drag you out of. There is nothing that would get me out of that cool stream of city=sanitized, low-lead, H2O. Zombies could be knocking at the door. The UPS guy or mailman could ring that doorbell. Heck, the back wall of the house could fall into a sinkhole. But I am enveloped in a cocoon of coolness that drains the heat of the day away. And I'm not coming out till I want to. Period.

Oh. What's that noise? Oh, it went away. Head back into the stream. Awwww. My heat-soaked body is beginning to cool down. Oh, there's that noise again. What the heck? It went away again. Sounded like someone was honking a horn out front. Who could that be? I left the phone on the bathroom counter. No noise from that. As I turn around, I try to do my best hair shake, and that horn honks again. Ok. What the heck is going on? I grab my large fluffy white towel, half-heartedly throw it around me, and head out into the living room. The pups come to greet me. Schipperkes love wet legs. And arms and hair. They diligently began drying those spots I had already serviced. I swear, I have no hair on the back of my calves thanks to my little Schipperdryers. I grab the blinds, slowly lift one of them up, and peer out. The neighbor walks by with her mini-Schnauzer. She looks right at me as I'm looking out at her. She starts walking faster. Our communications went downhill from there.

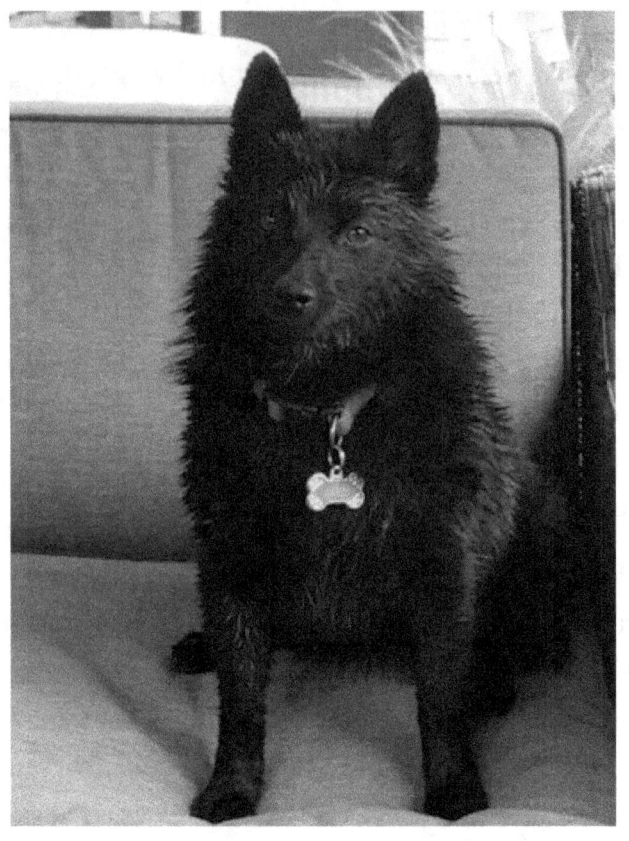

I wait thirty seconds as the Schipperdryers continue up my legs, licking the water as they go. I bend a blind and look. Nobody. Really? If I find out who disturbed my fortress of solitude, I will bury them in the desert beside an anthill. Reminds me of the good old days when I would light the paper bag on the neighbor's step, just to watch him come out, stomp on it, and go back in. Took years for me to find out I needed to load it with some puppy delights before I did it. Really, he wasn't a bad guy. Just didn't appreciate us sending baseballs over the fence at his car collection under covers. I didn't know. All I wanted to do was crush that ball.

I don't see the neighbor and I figure the religious folks have given up and moved on. The dogs have finished my calves and are working up. I head back to my fortress and back into the cool of the shower. Then all heck breaks loose. The horn starts honking with a familiar cadence. A familiar rhythm. Oh no. A familiar alarm. The keys. The dogs. OMG. The car alarm. The constant droning of the horn continues as I look out the bathroom window to the backyard. Coach and Luci are lying in the yard, close together. They are sharing the keyless entry fob for MY car. I grab the large fluffy white towel and head out of the bathroom at a panicked clip. I slide the glass door open and out into the 100-degree temperatures I fly. With a large fluffy white towel wrapped around me. Luci sees me first and grabs the fob. It is game on. Those that have tried to get a toy from a Schipperke have endured the "you can't catch me" syndrome. This is when a Schipperke gets something you want. And they know it. Schipperkes handle fast turns and high speed much better than a 58-year-old naked man, in a large fluffy white towel, fresh out of the shower. With bare feet.

The car alarm continues its beep, beep, beep sound, that by this time, had the neighbors wondering. She jinks left, then right. Then right under the large fluffy white towel away from me. She must have gotten tired of the heat and given up. In the house she goes, Coach close behind. The fob is in the backyard in pieces. The alarm continues beep, beep, beep. I think, thank goodness it's a Ford and not a foreign car. At least the horn sounds more pleasant. I go inside, still in my large fluffy white towel, and find my other set of keys. As I push the fob, nothing happens. The battery's dead.

Now, this horn has been going for more than a few minutes. It seems like hours to me. The only way you can disable an alarm is to go to the source and shut it off. In a large fluffy white towel, I open the front door and walk at a rather brisk pace, to my truck. I manually unlock it and hop in. The towel has issues. I start the truck and the alarm goes off. I shut it off, and in my large fluffy white towel, step out. As I lock the door, I swear I hear claps from my neighborhood. Nobody is standing on their porches, but I know. I know my large fluffy white towel is a winner that day. And so are Luci and Coach.

A LITTLE PERSONAL ABOUT ME

I have to admit my life hasn't been the best or the worst. I have seen both directions in my travels. Courtesy of the Air Force, I have been to England, Germany, Hawaii, Alaska, and Japan. And in the US, have hit just about every state, but for North Carolina and Maine. The military was, in retrospect, a major turning point in my life. And as I look back at it, I loved serving. Seriously. I made the best of the situation I was in. I had to get away.

My father was an amazing man. I know, most say that about their fathers. But my mom was more amazing. I was born in Ashton, Idaho in 1958. My mom, Florence, was a registered nurse in West Yellowstone. My father, Glynn (Dick) Richard, was a millwright at Yellowstone Lumber in West Yellowstone, Montana. We lived in a beautiful multi-story log cabin on the outskirts of town. Right by the airport. We didn't have a lot, but made due with what we had. We hunted, fished, and when necessary poached to put food on the table. I didn't know what beef was till I was 3 years old. Grandpa Lorenzo lived in Ashton, where he ran the Log Cabin Motel, now renamed Teton Mountain Inn.

Across the street, my Aunt Della and Uncle Steve ran the Ashton Motel. Down the street, R.J. Davis ran the gas station. It was a Davis kind of town. One of our true loves and passions was the day trip fishing. Before we went out fishing at Henrys Lake, we would get our daily supply of worms. We used to stick rods into the ground and power them up with 120 volts to coax the worms out of the ground. Boy, oh boy. They came in droves. But, one of my first life lessons was, don't run out into an electrified field of grass in bare feet in a diaper. I believe I soiled my diaper that day.

My gramps was a driver. He had a Scout that I swear, to this day, has the ability to bend and avoid trees. In Fremont County, we had roads, and then we had wood roads. Roads were to get to the wood roads. The wood roads were built only to remove timber from tracts of land that were inaccessible by any other means other than just pointing in a direction and going. They cut down only necessary timber to get to these places. So, you had to know which tree to turn at to follow these roads. Wood roads were for those not in their right minds. My gramps knew this country like the back of his hand. He loved the wood roads. So did my sister and I. Oh, I have a sister. Her name's Sandra. We used to be put in the back seat so we could become airborne projectiles as Gramps zigged and zagged through these stands of trees. Guess they figured we were safer back there, bouncing back and forth against the walls and roof, than where? LOL. Wood road 13 got us to a special place on the Henrys Fork of the Snake River. It had a big eddy that us kids could throw out a worm and marshmallow and catch something. Something being 2- and 3-pound trout. We would fill the cooler and before dark make our way back to civilization. Gramps would run that road from dry to feet of mud just to get us to that special spot.

Sadly, my dad contracted polio and lost the use of his legs. We lined up like little soldiers to take our polio vaccination and my dad was one to react adversely to it. We moved to Ashton for a while, but ended up in Boise, Idaho because we had access to the Veterans Hospital. My dad was also a veteran. And my grampa was also a veteran. A long line of veterans. I'm still humbled when I hear the Star Spangled Banner and cry when I hear "God Bless the U.S.A." by Lee Greenwood. And I admit I get real annoyed when someone doesn't respect the flag and what it stands for. Ok, off the soapbox.

We moved around Boise as I was growing up and settled on an acre and a half in East Boise. We built a big sloping patio so that Dad could run around the property in his wheelchair. But Dad just didn't handle being in a wheelchair well. He became withdrawn and when he talked, he lashed out. I love my sister and my mom. And I took the brunt of Dad's anger about his situation, to protect my mom and sister. But the time came I had to get away, too. I joined the Air Force in 1978. Our basic training flight was an Honor Flight. I got to tech school at Chanute AFB in Illinois. Graduated an Honor Graduate. I sucked jet engines up. I was stationed at Little Rock AFB in Arkansas. In 1981, I came home for Christmas.

On December 28, 1981, my father passed away with heart failure. I was up at Bogus Basin that day, snow skiing with one of my best friends, Mike Collins. I wasn't staying at home, but with a friend. Vally was her name. I stayed there because I was strong enough to say no to my dad's verbal abuse. I was old enough to walk away. And man enough to avoid putting myself into a confrontational situation. I was home to see my mom.

When we got to her house, she said I needed to call my sister. I knew, in my heart, that this was the day of release for all of us. Release for me, for the years of physical abuse I had endured. Release for my sister for the same. And, for my mom, release from the physical and emotional abuse she had endured over all those years. My mom was alone on an acre and a half of land with a 2,600-square foot home. I spent thirty days with her, then I had to go back to Arkansas. That hurt me deeply.

I ended my active duty in 1982 because I felt I needed to be there to help my mom on the property. I wasn't the best son. The house and property were more than I could handle at that time in my life. But I tried. I joined the Air Guard for two years to fulfill my military requirement, but my heart is and always will be with my brothers and sisters in arms. I am a United States Air Force veteran. And I stand proud.

The last picture you see in this chapter is of my mom. This is the last time she really got out and had fun at the Western Idaho State Fair. And this is one of the last pictures I treasure of her before she passed March 12, 2017.

IT'S TIME FOR A TRIP

I went through a lot of tears and anguish when I had to send Sasha and Gizmo across Rainbow Bridge in 2016. It affected me in ways that left me despondent and unattached from my friends and life in general. This picture of her is the day I sent her across the bridge.

My heart still hurts that I had to do that, but I knew that look in her eyes. That look of, "Dad, it's ok. I'll be waiting for you on the other side." I only pray that I get that chance to see my babies again. And my mom. And my grandpa. I decided it was time to take a trip to release the demons that had haunted me for so many years. But I had new fur kids – Luci, my four-year-old retired show Schip, that was just happy with a captive audience of love; and Coach, also a retired show dog, but from Colorado. He would assume a position of comfort on the opposite side of me for the hands of love. These two fur kids had saved me from a shortened life, but I still needed to get away and just be alone to reflect on my life in the past and for the future. Who could I trust to take care of two new-to-the-family Schipperkes, that would bolt for freedom at a second's notice. In came a very special lady and family.

I knew of Tammy through one of my closest friends, Brandon. I met Brandon years back at a small asphalt racetrack called Meridian Speedway. I had been going since the '70s and had my established parking place for my butt. Everyone knew not to invade my butt space or face the wrath of the grouchy old man. But I was only in my 20s, 30s, 40s, and 50s. Yes, I have been going to this track for over three decades. Brandon's always sat lower to the right of me and I have my perch at the top of the bleachers, where I can see everything that goes on. An old veteran thing. Grab the high ground and they have to come up to get ya. Lol. Brandon and I share a lively banter about the track, drivers, and wrecks. But yelling over the cars makes it difficult.

One day, I invited him up to my perch to lean against the back fence and relax. A few barley pops later, the races were just a distraction for our conversation, that took on a life of its own. We talked about everything. And found out that we shared a lot in common. I had found a friend. Over the years, we developed that relationship into a brotherhood. I was there most weekends, just chilling and enjoying the company. He helped me through the

break-up of a seven-year relationship. He was there when I needed a friend, confidant, and a carpenter/handyman. He was there when few would take that time. I trusted him with everything, except my Schipperkes.

Now, if you have bought this book, you know about the trust issues Schipperke owners have when it comes to their fur kids. I'm about the most trusting guy in the world. Call me gullible or call me a man with a gentle heart that would give the shirt off his back to cover a stranger. I have been taken advantage of and I have called it a life lesson. I have lost money and tools to those that I trusted. But I no longer hold anger for their actions or any remorse for doing what they did. Let God sort it out. I'm just trying to put more in the plus bracket than in the negative bracket. I couldn't think of anyone that I would trust with my babies. Therefore, I wasn't going anywhere.

Life as a Schipperke Owner | 63

We were having a get together for New Year's Eve at a piano bar downtown. Dueling pianos sounded fun and dinner was served, so I was in. Brandon said his mom wanted to come and I thought, sure. Let the young kids play as us old folks sit to the side and watch. I had met Tammy before at Brandon's and hadn't really thought there was a spark. We both had our issues and I just didn't want to be hurt anymore. I was resigned to being single for my remaining years on Mother Earth. I just wanted to have a good night and to say 2017, here we come. We got a party van to transport us to and from our homes so that we didn't have to worry about our level of sobriety. The evening was very enjoyable, but it was hard to talk when singing with the whole bar. We started seeing each other and my shield started to drop. We started hanging out and I found I came to trust her. Trust is a finicky thing when it comes to emotions. I trusted her. But with my Schipperkes? I needed a test drive.

As a responsible Schipperke owner, you have to vet everyone that may come in contact with your fur kids. I interviewed her mom and sister at length and did a few test runs with the fur kids over there. I walked the perimeter and checked out the fences for security. Each and every picket because it was single picket only. I considered asking that they put pickets on the other side to double up the escape protection, but reconsidered. I went around to the gates and checked the security of the locks and hinges to make sure it didn't just fall down in a tornado. We don't have tornadoes in Idaho. Just microbursts. I checked the doors inside and out for security, and the security system.

Now, I'm a trusting guy. Except when it comes to my fur kids. I tend to be a little over the top with them. We had no issues with our initial contacts and the dogs loved running in this big water-laden backyard. Luci ran with wild abandon up and down the stream that led into the ponds full of Koi. She splashed around like a kid in a candy store. They loved being over there. Things were fine. Till the day. That day. Tammy had dealt with my request of getting locks on the gates to prevent someone from coming in and leaving the gate open. Not locks, just hooks that prevented the gate from opening till you got to the front door. Security. I had bought porta fences that gave a secondary wall in front of the gates, just in case someone came in and the dogs were out and about. But that day will go down in infamy. It was the day of the Great Escape.

Tammy and I were about to leave when I saw this black streak run across the street, headed to parts unknown. I screamed in my best female voice, "What the heck is going on?"

Replace words as necessary. Tammy's sister Becky had left the gate open. Luci saw freedom. And when Becky opened the garage door, there went the fur kid. As I yelled in Yiddish, some very bad words, I took off, at my best trot, after a dog that was fully capable of running circles around me.

You already know, as I have said before, that you should not chase Schipperkes. But I was in my normal Schipper panic mode. Run fast, yell stupid things, and watch the dog run off into the sunset. Thankfully, Luci ran into the corner of a yard where she realized she was caught. She just sat down and waited for me.

The trust was broken for weeks. I had to do my rounds each time someone moved into the outer reaches of the yard. The gates. The garage. I was a silent shadow, walking behind others to assure the security of my fur kids. After a few months of retraining, my trust level had returned. Somewhat. I asked Tammy if she would take care of my kids while I went on a walkabout. A journey of rediscovery. A soul search. She said yes, she would babysit my kids while I went on my vacation. I made reservations and dropped the kids off. After a lot of Schipperlove, I walked away from my babies. It hurt, but it felt empowering. I could do things without my dogs. I got to the airport and hopped on a plane to the Florida Keys.

As soon as I got off the plane, I texted, asking how the kids were. Tammy said, "They are fine."

I slept well that night. Because I trusted. The next morning, I texted Tammy, asking, "How are the kids?"

"They are fine," came the reply again. I spent the day just reading and watching the tide roll in and out.

That night, over 2,000 miles away, I learned to trust. Tammy had my fur kids and, if something happened, I knew she would handle it. But they were my fur kids. I spent the next six days just cruising up and down the Florida Keys. I went to Key West and kicked the rock. I ate some amazing seafood. I ate some amazing prime rib. But each night I texted Tammy. How are the kids? They are fine. When I got home, I cried. I reached down and grabbed my Schips and I cried. I saw the sun set on my past. And I saw the sun rise on my future. And I was humbled by the fact that Tammy, Luci, and Coach were a part of my life.

SCHIPPERLAB

Most of those that are around Schipperkes learn about the history of the breed. Partially because we have to explain to everyone we show a picture to, what they are. Partially because we want to know what we just got ourselves into.

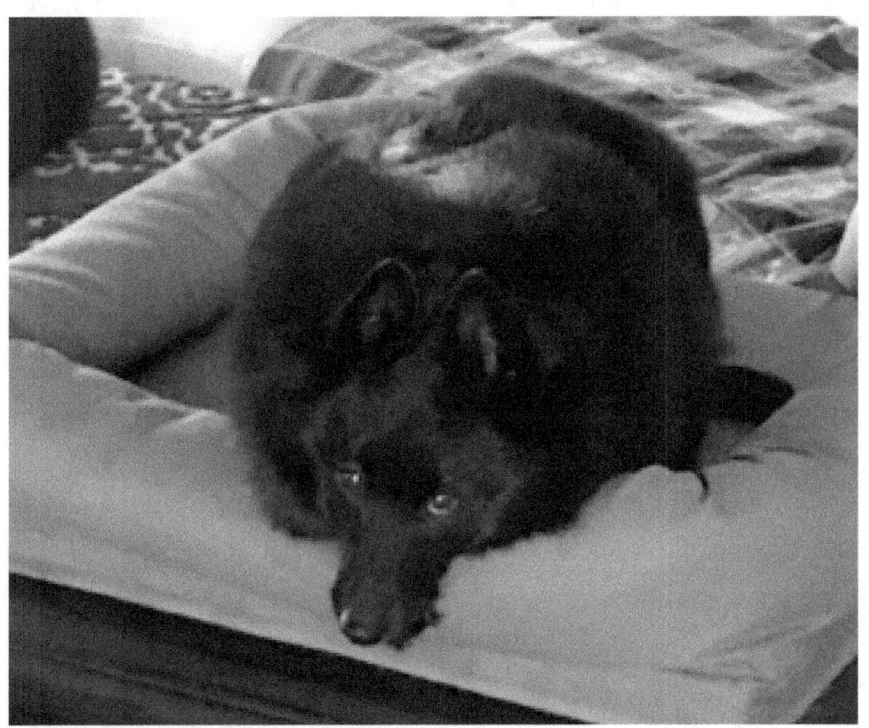

They originated in Belgium in the 16th century. The debate goes on whether they are from Spitz or Sheepdog blood. Their temperament ranges from confident to curious. Faithful to fearless. Independent and alert. I have heard stories they were bred to be rat dogs on tugs and barges. And due to their unrelenting desire to get whatever they are digging for, they have been known to show up in China after a few days of digging. They are interested in everything around them and will investigate even the smallest movements. Do not move your toes at night.

Luci and Coach take different outlooks on life. Coach is the laid-back big male dog that just wants to get along with everyone. He prefers a comfortable couch or a warm back porch to searching out the yard for a rogue grasshopper to attack. He enjoys lying next to you at night and serenading you with snores. I have personally seen the curtains move on a warm night, but that could be the breeze. Coach loves just about everyone. There are a few people he is wary of and those are the people that make a lot of noise. The plumber, electrician, floor-laying guys. The UPS and FedEx delivery guys. And some strangers. But, for the most part, he is a very mellow dog that just wants belly scratches and a warm place to sleep.

Enter Luci. She goes from zero to obscene speeds within seconds and is quite the little zoomer dog. She gets into a large space and the first thing she does is kick in that overdrive. Around and around the yard she goes, checking everything out at high speed. She has time to check it out later at reduced speeds. But, for now, she smokes around the perimeter of the yard scoping out her venue.

Luci and Coach both are leash-only dogs when we are in public. They lead relatively well, being retired show dogs. But they are constantly challenging me with the faster, faster, faster thing. We have all had that dog that slowly speeds up till you are wondering if you are on a walk or in a marathon. I have run with Luci. And she gets up to my speed, which is an advanced walk and not a run, and seems happy to just run next to me. She looks over and I can see it in her eyes: "Come on old man. Get with it."

It's enjoyable running with a dog. Schipperkes are an exception. Just as you get your rhythm, have your feet lifting enough not to trip, and start to enjoy it, they hit the parking brakes. Squirrel. The word that sends every Schip into a frothy frenzy of barking and tree climbing. They will cross a four-lane highway with wild abandon to see a squirrel in a tree a half mile away. Squirrels are the primary reason I don't run on the greenbelt in our city. Boise has the Boise River that runs down the middle of it. There are thousands of majestic trees along this river. And there are squirrels. There are hundreds of them and they are capable of strategic assaults on humans and dogs at any time. You always think they are in those maple trees throwing nut shells at you by accident. Think again. They sit up there and talk to each other. Yes, full-blown conversations about how to trip up the runner or knock the random biker from their two-wheeled steed. They send a sacrificial runner as a decoy, then a couple more to finish the carnage. Before you know it, there's a pile of people and bikes spread across a large area after they avoided hitting or running over a poor squirrel. Some call them rats with tails. I call them geniuses. They get humans to feed them. They have unlimited water from the river. And they get exercise each day running across the greenbelt when two dogs are walking by.

We all remember the game Twister. You contort your body based on colors on a slick piece of plastic. You get two dogs, on leads, going in opposite directions, chasing multiple squirrels, and there you have a massive pile-up. By the time they are safely back in the trees, the bodies are just finishing piling up. Then they sit up there and mock everyone with laughs and giggles as the humans try to get everything untangled. I can't figure out if people are afraid of hurting them or afraid of being attacked. But, when you see a squirrel, trust me, they are up to something no good. Luci loves to run around Tammy's backyard. She has also developed a habit of running up and down the stream that feeds into one of the ponds. This makes me wonder, is my Schipperke part Lab?

Really, this dog will get into the backyard when the sprinklers are on. She will go challenge those sprinklers to a duel. Her mouth against the sprinkler head. And these are vicious sprinkler heads. They have some power behind them. But it's well water so I just look at them as a large water pick for her teeth. She will run up and bite at the heads and stream until she's totally soaked. We all know where a wet Schip ends up. Right in your lap or on the sofa next to you. Look at that face. Really? Could you just push away your dog when they look like that?

I have a back-up plan when I'm over there. I carry towels and place them around the property. I am prepared. Luci thinks it is really cool to go visit her Koi. There are two 3,500-gallon ponds with habitat and stream. These Koi are worth some bling bling. In the summer, they hide at the bottom of the ponds, where it's coolest. But they seem to have a relationship with my water dog. She will get into the pond where there's a ledge and gently paw the water. The Koi will come up and say hello. Then she will get out and run up and down the stream. I haven't seen it happen yet, but I know she will have an accident. One day she will not stop fast enough at the end of the stream. Splashdown?

Schips can swim, can't they? See, we are going to rebuild the stream this spring. It's pretty shallow right now. But I put a Tim-Allen, more-horsepower pump into the system and we now have Niagara River flowing into the ponds. Tammy wasn't impressed when I had to get into the breaker panel and upgrade the breakers. I was going to take the dryer and oven breakers out, but thought otherwise. My health is important to me, even in these later years. And you don't mess with the oven. I figured, that's why they have main breakers in the panel. I upgraded from 1/3 hp to 1 1/2 hp on the big pond with the stream. It looked amazing. Over twice the volume. My limit was pipe diameter. But I made it work. Then I whined till Tammy relented and said yes to a new pump on the waterfall pond. I felt empowered. And a little warped.

We remember the evil Wicked Witch of the West from The Wizard of Oz? I was the other one. I was rubbing my hands together in joy. But I needed a better waterfall. My dogs demanded it. Back I headed to my go-to site. amazon.com. Lol. No kickbacks on there. But that's where I got a steal on my last pump. The old pump was also a 1/3 hp pump. Both were over ten years old, so they were just worn out. The perfect time to bring in the big guns.

Now, I had Brandon – Tammy's son and my close friend – come over and replace the outlet before I got the other pump. The outlet had seen better years. And it was falling apart. He asked me about the pump. I said it was a little bigger. Just a little. Not much, but the price was right. I snuck it right by Tammy and Brandon that day. I lulled them into a false sense of, "I know what I'm doing," and that night I pushed the purchase button. I was giddy and excited because this would look beautiful when that torrent was flowing out of that fall and it would help oxygenate the water. Lol. I got a bigger pump.

Now, as I waited, like a kid with a new toy, for my pump, I focused my attention to the stream and pond I had just upgraded. My new concern was that the dogs would get flushed down the stream when they jumped in. Ok, one Schipperke in particular. Luci. My Schipperlab. She loved the increased flow. She ran with wild abandon up and down the stream. She was in Schipperke water heaven. Coach made a few efforts to follow her, but she was fearless. Coach was Coach. I had to dip him in the pond every so often to keep him cool. I swear he peed on something valuable to me, each time I did that. My keys. My flip-flops. A few days later, I got the second pump. It was only 1 hp, but I knew after I saw the stream flow in the other pond, that this would be perfect. Brandon had replaced the plug-in, so I was good to go. Just a few cuts on hoses and some adapters. I finished wiring the pump and I was ready for the moment. I envisioned Luci under the waterfall and playing in the stream. Like a black-haired beauty under the waterfall, shaking her hair. Coach was on the sofa. I hit the switch on the back of the pump and it went dark. Everything stopped. Oops. Houston, we have a problem.

I heard a sizzle in the box where Brandon had been and went to investigate. Seems there was just a tad too little space in the box and two wires joined the party together. The breaker didn't appreciate that and shut everything off. Simple fix. Normally, duct tape would be the weapon of choice, but today, I went with a fresh roll of electrical tape. Duct tape, for those in the know, is electrically conductive. Don't use it for powered applications. That's my disclaimer. I wrapped one layer. Two layers. What the heck. After half a roll, I felt comfortable with the insulating properties of the tape. I stuffed it back in the box and screwed it tight. Back to the breaker panel for round two. I tripped it and nothing happened. That is, nothing bad. I went back out and the big pump was chugging along. I hopped in and flipped the switch. Everything went dark. Oops. What the heck had happened now?

I got out my trusty iPhone and went to the calculator. Now, I am not an electrician. I never aspired to be or wanted to be. But I'm not uneducated in the electrical sciences. I just choose not to be randomly zapped till I have an accident in my drawers. I hate being zapped. It's unpredictable and therefore does not belong in my life. I hate being zapped. Coach was on the sofa. Luci was playing in the pond. I hate being zapped. That being said, I looked up the amperage draws of both super pumps and realized. I needed more power. That oven was looking pretty good for a circuit because they use it less than the dryer. I went in and pulled the panel face and found my problem. There was only a 20 amp breaker on my circuit.

Now, I looked at the panel. In theory, you should never exceed the maximum of the panel with breakers. That is, if you have everything in the house on at the same time, the system should be set up to handle it. All I needed was 10 amps. I headed to the local Grover's electrical store and grabbed a 30 amp breaker. No, no, no. Go big or go home? That's what I heard. I went for a 40 amp breaker. I got back and the dogs were wondering where I had gone to. Coach went to the sofa. Luci, well. The stream was dry. The waterfall wasn't working. She was talking to the Koi. I hate getting zapped. And here I go again. Into the main electrical panel to replace the problem breaker. I had this vision that they would pry my fried body off the panel and then start the dryer and bake a cake. I waded in and managed to get it replaced without getting zapped. Did I mention, I hate getting zapped. I went out to the pumps and plugged them in. I think that the lights in the neighborhood may have dimmed a little bit, but eureka. The falls fell. The stream streamed. And the ponds ... well, they ponded.

Coach was on the sofa panting. I was elated. I was so excited to show the new look to the family. I dipped Coach into the pond and he was trash grunting me the whole way. My Coach grunts. It is such a neat sound. When he is happy, he grunts. Today he was happy to be dunked. And they were happy with the look.

NEVER TRUST A DELIVERY GUY

From December 26, 2017:

So, we all have been rooting and praying for Thistle Weed to be returned safely home after his escape and adventure. Thankfully, he was returned home this morning thanks to a very caring stranger. But, I had my own little adventure this morning.

I had delivery of my new bedroom set from Mor Furniture this morning. When I was contacted, I told the leader of this rat pack that I had some instructions for them before they entered my remodel project. As they pulled up, I went out and swept the deicer off the driveway and sidewalk. I had moved the runners into the living room and hallway to keep the mess off my new carpet in the living room. The dogs were barking. I told them that my two Schipperkes were friendly and very valuable to me.

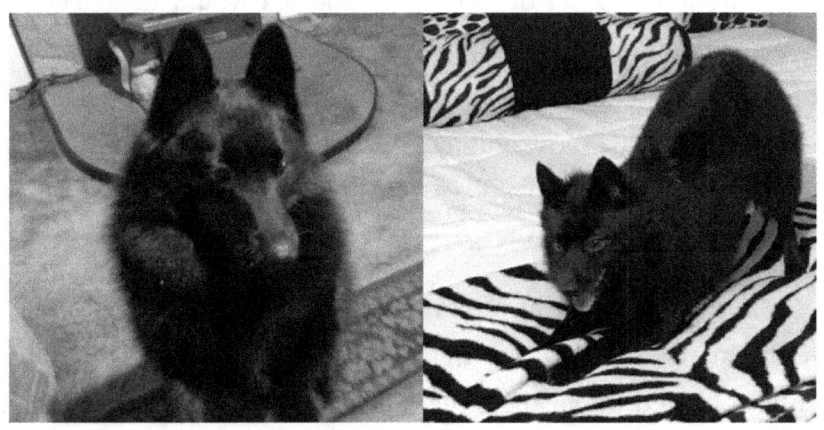

The dogs were barking and scratching at the windows. I then told them that I would remove the dog door insert in my back sliding glass door and put the dogs outside while they were moving stuff in. Two of them walked by me with a headboard. The dogs trying to tear blinds off windows and barking. I walked in the door and grabbed Coach and headed towards the glass door to remove the dog door. As I pushed Luci out, she came in the dog door and headed around the corner. I had to put Coach down to pull the insert and around the corner he went. Just then, my world went into an emotional and verbal turmoil.

I ran around the corner in socks and saw the front door open and the dogs heading out into the general public, free to run without the restraints of collars or their slave walker. Out the door I went, in my socks, running after the dogs, yelling things I can't post. I told them to drop that headboard and get those dogs. Of course, the dogs, seeing that I had reinforcements, split up and went in separate directions. The verbal abuse continued as I yelled at two to go after Luci and I would go after Coach. They were running through 6 inches of snow so normally I would stand a chance to catch them rather quickly. I was wearing socks though. As most of you know, socks offer little or NO traction in the house, let alone in the street with snow and ice. As I yelled out instructions like a drill sergeant, I ran towards Coach and loudly spoke words he has never listened to. DOWN!!!!!!!!!

He froze as I have never spoken to him with more than a normal voice. I snatched him up and turned around. My feet were cold. I looked down the street and saw Luci doing her best ice skating moves down the street towards Curtis. A major street also covered with ice. As I slid up to the door to deposit Coach in the house, I grabbed the screen door handle and yanked it open. Somehow the latch had locked and, when I pulled, it tore the frame loose and broke the handle. Did I mention my feet were ice cubes by this point? I put Coach in and closed the front door. The screen was dangling by a chain and a few screws.

Out across the yard, and into the street I went. I yelled at the fast kid to try to pass her up and redirect her back towards us. Now, I don't know if this kid has ever been in the Olympics, but he passed Luci up with the speed of Bolt. He put on the brakes like a semi in full lock-up, and Luci just stopped. Right there in the middle of the street. Just stood there. I yelled Luci in my best "don't sound panicked" voice. And she headed right back down the street, across the 6 inches of snow in the front yard, and up to me. She bowed down and I scooped her up. And I kissed and hugged her like as if I hadn't seen her in months.

My socks were frozen to the patio. My feet were somewhere in the Ice Age they were so cold. I managed to peel the socks loose and got her into the house. As I closed the door, I asked everyone to stop moving for a minute and to listen to me. I apologized for my behavior and the threats of physical harm to them. I also apologized for the tirade of language that had come out of my mouth, as I was under duress. I went inside, removed the dog door and put the dogs outside. I went in and sat down on the sofa to catch my breath. My feet were cold. The dogs were barking. The delivery guys were standing outside the door. Not moving. Not an inch. I guess I scared them. Lol.

Me, an old man, with a couple of little dogs. No way. I opened the door and said it was safe. They came in tentatively at first, keeping a very close eye on me. And I think they may have broken a record for the fastest putting together of a bedroom set. I sat on the sofa and warmed my feet. The dogs barked. As they were leaving, I again apologized for the threats to their manly parts and shook their hands. I thanked them for helping me get my dogs back. And watched as they fishtailed that big truck down the street in what seemed to be a hurry.

The bedroom set looked great. The front screen door needed replaced and the dogs, they were right there sleeping blissfully. As if nothing had ever happened.

SCHIPPERVIZING THE REMODEL

Now, as some of my Schipperke family know, I have been in the laborious task of remodeling my thirty-year-old home. The reason for the purge is twofold. Number one is that my house is thirty years old. It deserves an upgrade just in case I prematurely pass on to the other side. The bank and my family deserve better.

The second reason is more important. It's to purge the evil spirits of past relationships that tend to drag you into the past and force you to relive those heartbreaking times and experiences. Each time I walked into my master bedroom, I regressed back years to the time my then wife decided that it needed to look like The Wizard of Oz. Complete with green walls, tapestry, and pictures of The Wizard of Oz. Maybe she wasn't aspiring to be a witch, but I slept with one eye open just in case. We had an overabundance of brooms located in closets and nooks around the house. But, in her defense, she made a pretty sexy witch each year for Halloween. I never thought of connecting the dots.

My last relationship lasted seven years. And, ladies, hang on to the following words and gasp in utter amazement. I am a man.

But I am human. I made mistakes that destroyed my relationship with an amazing woman. And at the same time, I hurt her deeply. I couldn't find a way to give that love I had inside to her with the commitment she needed. I didn't nourish that love she was trying so hard to give me. I realized I had internal issues that needed help. And yes, I got help. But at the cost of my relationship. And each day I struggle with the few demons that pop up. But I'm trying. As evidenced by my past benevolence, I have no shortage in the heart and soul department. I have problems trusting and giving freely all the love that's in my heart. Call me a work in progress. But I have digressed enough. I've always wanted to say that. Lol.

I was in a rut and needed a life change in my house. I went and bought a pallet of laminate for the whole interior of the house. Enough of that thirty-year-old carpet. And with seven dogs, two kids and a grease monkey over those thirty years, the carpet was toast. I started throwing everything out. The bed. The dressers. The stools, chairs, anything that wasn't tied to the floor. This was an environmental purge. And it was refreshing. Some call it minimization. Making your life as simple as possible with minimal clutter. I was becoming the king of my domain again. Oops. When done in the proper order, it's good. And I have to admit, my sofa was pretty comfortable. It was over-width and if you took the back pillows, you had a full-on 8-foot twin in the living room. It was a little old, so I had to reinforce the cushions with some plywood to avoid sinking onto the floor each night. Yes, I said each night. That became my new bedroom for a few months.

The Schipperkids were not impressed at first. But they grew into it. Luci would wrap around my head and Coach would take up the space between the edge and me. One happy family. Now some of these pictures may seem shocking for some. But, let's work through this together. I started in the master bedroom. After throwing everything out, I tore up the carpet, pad, base, and door mouldings.

Now, this would normally be an easy project, unless you also have two Schipperkes to contend with. I have to admit that they were most effective helpers when it came to the pad. Schips being diggers just jumped right in and tore it up after I uncovered it. It was rather entertaining to watch. However, I need to teach them to pull out the staples and tack strips next time. They would lay in the hallway as I worked, taking in the smells and sounds. That is until I made a noise with something larger than a screwdriver. Coach didn't like loud noises. As I was tearing out the trim and staples off the floor, he assumed a place of comfort. On the back patio. And there was snow on it. Down the hallway I worked. It came to a point where I needed my Schipperkids to stay out of the construction zone, so I blocked them off.

For a few days. Brandon and I laid laminate in the master bedroom and down the hallway. And then freedom. I had bought runners with the fur kids in mind, but didn't get them down in time. They had to check out the new smells and floor. I pulled back the gate and before I had it to the side, there they went, scurrying by. Things were fine when they were on the carpet. But they were suddenly confronted with a new challenge. Traction. I take care of my kids' nails. Each month, I take them in and they get a trim. I would not try this. Nail trimming is not in my pay scale or job description. As they started down the hallway, the pitter-patter of little paws turned to more intense movement. Then, they both seemed to look at each other as if to say, "Game on." I saw it. Plain and simple. Luci gave Coach a butt shove and it was game on.

Now Coach outweighs Luci by 8 pounds. In human standards, 8 pounds is nothing. But by Schipperke standards, it's like a quarterback against a lineman. Weight wins every time. Coach slides to the side a little but picks up the pace. He takes the inside line, then hits the gas. I'm standing back watching what might be a serious crash and burn at the end of the hallway. But they both were determined to be first through the bedroom door to grace the virgin territory. New smells. New areas to explore. The excitement for them was at the top of the scale. The terror for me and the vet were up there, too.

They hit the end of the hallway at full speed and there was no way they would make the corner. Coach was digging for traction as he hit Luci. Luci was along for the ride then. They both went down in a pile of fur and claws. They slid the final few feet, and bang, into the wall at the hallway end. Then, a miracle occurred. We all have seen it. Schipperkes are notorious for this and each time I see it, I'm overcome with amazement. They both popped up and stood there like nothing had just happened. "We had it under control the whole time," they seemed to say. "That big pile of fur at the end of the hallway was an illusion. A figment of human imagination."

They walked, in step, together into the bedroom. I ran back there thinking I needed to take one or both to the ER. Something had to give as I headed down the hallway in my socks. I wear socks a lot, when I'm in the house, to keep my feet warm. The dogs destroyed my lambskin slippers, so I'm forced to run around in socks. Socks offer warmth, but little traction.

I built up speed on the carpet and as I hit the laminate I realized one fatal mistake. I weigh in at 190 pounds. And I'm not in bad shape, given my life in racing and other self-abusive legal physical activities. But, even I can't change Einstein's laws. That is what is in motion, will stay in motion, till compelled to change from outside sources or objects.

Ok, I could quote the rules that were about to apply to my situation, but we all know what was about to happen.

I hit the laminate and immediately realized that I had no traction. And the walls were looming. I made a last-ditch effort to grab the bathroom door opening that sent me into a helpless spin. I hit the floor and slid to a stop in a pile at the end of the hall. My Schipper medics came to the rescue. In they came. As I lay there, Luci crawled onto my chest and Coach lay down next to me. They both licked my wounds.

I slowly gathered myself and wondered, How does something so small, manage to be so tough? And tender? Well, I'm not quite that tough.

The next day, my fur kids were right there checking me out as I plugged away on the remodel. I had Aleve and they had extra snacks. The old bed/sofa's gone and a new one's now in place. But that floor looks good. And there are a lot of runners down to avoid another wreck at the end of the hallway.

THINGS THAT HAPPEN AT CAMP STAY AT...

I was proud of my abilities in my younger years. I was athletic. I could outpace the neighborhood bully on my single-speed Schwinn on any given day. I was smart. I could find the most strategic ways to remove apples from the neighbors' trees without anyone knowing. And the other neighbors' cherry trees. And the other neighbors' pear trees. You get it.

My childhood was filled with glorious fruits and very annoyed neighbors. I thought it was the responsible thing to do, after partaking in the fruits, to return the remainder to the yard I had got them from. Call it reseeding for next year. My best summer memories were in my teens at a place called Camp Billy Rice in the central mountains of Idaho. The Boy Scout Encampment took over the major portion of lakeside property on Warm Lake. Why they called it Warm Lake, I have no idea.

Approaching the lake gave you a sense of foreboding. The water was crystal clear because the inflows were fresh from the mountain snows that accumulate over the winter. But that makes it rather cool to the nether regions of one's body. And it challenges one to jump towards the wild side. Take a chance. Run down that 50-foot pier and just jump into that beautiful clear water. We reveled in challenging new packs, that would come in each week, to the pier challenge. And stood back marveling at those silly newcomers that dared to run and jump. I believe, to this day, there are kids still frozen in ice at the bottom of that lake. We were camp cooks for a summer and we spent the summer up in those mountains.

Each morning we were awoken by the most responsible adult or kid, depending on the day. The weekends tended to be kind of rough on the adults. Something about drinking to cope. We never really understood. We would trudge up to the mess hall, from our humble commode, and proceeded to put out the most amazing layout of fruits, vegetables, and bacon anyone but a Scout had ever seen. More on the commode later. Hold your breath. I was very good at bacon. That was my passion. The eggs were too sensitive for my manly hands. They broke too easily. And every Scout wanted over easy. I couldn't handle the pressure of trying to flip those on a consistent basis. I was good for scrambled though. The pancakes were a subject of contention amongst our group. Pancakes are pancakes. It's the color that sent us into a quandary. Honestly, what is the difference between black and dark brown? It's all in the lighting. And if only one side was black and the other side raw, does it even out to light brown? And if it's black on the side you can't see, is it ok? Really, who would dare to flip their pancake stack in the middle of a line of 300 hungry Boy Scouts?

We had a couple of rogues challenge the kitchen cooks. They are still at peace in a shallow grave next to the dumpster. That is, only if the bears didn't get them. We will never know. The bacon. It was an art. A science. A skill that few will ever achieve and even fewer will ever really make it to the Baconator level. I was the master Baconator. I was the kitchen master of pork. The top porker of all I surveyed. Pork-wise. I could take a slab of pork and turn it into a Picasso. I could make it melt in your hungry little Scout mouths. They would stand in line for my bacon. And maybe the pancakes and eggs. But my bacon was king in the kitchen. They were considering a bacon master merit badge just for me, but sadly, it was shot down by the vegans.

Each day, we would toil in the obscure depths of the kitchen to provide sustenance for all those starving Scouts that had been out on so many adventures around our massive camp. Without us. Three meals a day. Just after breakfast, we prepped for a simple lunch. Then dinner was a mega course of multicultural delights that would challenge even the most finicky of palettes. Not. Burnt chicken. Burnt beef. Not steaks. We made efforts to make the hamburger look like steak. Burnt. We were so good at breakfast, but lunch and dinner were marginal at best. But the condiments were such an amazing sight to behold. The onions and tomatoes were carefully sliced. The pickles were pickles. The buns were buns. Some of our Scouts received a little more penicillin than anyone else. I'll leave it at that. Each was carefully laid out to perfection. And there was ham. I was good at sliced ham. But, each afternoon, after the kitchen was abused, destroyed, and cleaned up to hospital cleanliness standards, we, the kitchen staff were let loose.

In retrospect, I look at what I did as indentured servitude. But at those times in our lives, we want to venture out. To spread our wings. To spend a summer free of the adult constraints that prevented us from doing stupid stuff. Yea. Stupid stuff. I honestly believe in my heart that we were the inventors of the zip line. Really. As Boy Scouts, you are taught to be creative. To think outside the box. To go where no Scout has gone before. Oops. Trademark infringement? Nope. We started small with stuff we rounded up from the camp. Some rope. Some old shirts and gloves. Each day, the excitement built. We got the line up. Then we test-drove it with a shirt. The elevation change wasn't sufficient to get any real speed. It was more dragging feet and pushing.

The next try was better. We started low and ended up high. In the trees. The drop wasn't too bad. As long as you could crawl down the tree trunk. Our first aid cabinet needed frequent refills of triple antibiotic ointment for some reason. The counselors were getting suspicious. We needed another ending to our zip-line journeys. Something that didn't involve a bearhug on a pine tree 15 feet in the air. Followed by a drop to the ground and skid marks on your thighs. Triple antibiotic ointment. Our hooch, look that up, was a two-room cabin. The adults slept in comfort in one room. And four of us, 15-year-old, wild and crazy males, were in the other. We longed for adventure. And we were determined to find a way to get in trouble. And have adventures. After the counselors saw our genius design, they decided we needed to direct our enthusiasm in another direction.

That night, we had a compound incursion. In the middle of the night, we were awakened by a sound that came from what sounded like the dumpster. We had no windows on that side of the cabin, so in adult childlike sounds, we managed to wake up the snoring adults in the next room. It may have had something to do with the "Oh my god, we are being attacked!" sounds that came from somewhere around our room. They knocked on our door and we all cowered in the corners of our bunks. "Sasquatch is outside and we are so dead!"

There may have been some screams, too. Not me. Then, the voice of reason came through. We heard a familiar voice and opened the door. Our adult pointed to the black thing hanging in the dumpster with two legs flailing in the air. The steel lid was laid over that creature's back and it looked like it was in distress. Can't get out, can't get in. Quandary. As we watched, it became apparent it was a black bear getting in the dumpster to relieve us of all those nasty pancakes and eggs. Maybe some leftovers from lunch and dinner. My bacon was absent. It was too good. We stood in awe as it wriggled around, never going in or coming out. Just hanging there. The challenge was thrown out to go up and spank it. But that was quickly quenched by someone far more intelligent than us. As we were reassured that the black bear was far more interested in the contents of the dumpster than us, we went back to the cabin. But the brains were in fluidic motion. Tomorrow. We will build an escape line. But it must be done covertly. We all slept with one eye open. The next day, we got to the engineering of a new, more effective means of escaping a bear attack. The frontal assault surely would end in our demise. We needed a secondary escape route just in case the black bear decided we were a late-night snack. Outside our rear window was a perfect sight line to the lake. Warm Lake. But, it was our protection and salvation in the event of that inevitable black bear assault.

We did our service to the kitchen and immediately started to build the escape route. The rope was too flimsy. We started digging around the outbuildings and found some new toys. Quarter-inch cable with attaching hardware. And the pulleys with it. We were in engineering heaven. There was no way even a hungry bear was going to catch us once we punched the button and launched down that cable. Covertly, we hung a cable between two big pines about 5 feet from the lake. About 15 feet in the air. Then, we did the same at the top. But only 8 feet in the air.

Ok, you all know where this is going. Even though you can't see the flight path, use your imagination. The cabins sit over 50 feet above the lake level. Putting the cable 15 feet in the air left us with a nice gentle glide slope to the lake. We would be up in the air, but would just let go and land on the ground and stop before the lake. Engineering at its best. Covertly. In order to accomplish this, we had to do this in steps, over many days, in the darkness. It had to be high enough to not draw any scrutiny from those adult figures. But be accessible to us. There was no test drive on this. No way. The only way you would need this escape system is if your life was in jeopardy. And we were living on the edge each night. I began throwing food in the dumpster to combat the inevitable meeting with that black bear. We tried to deter him. But every other night he would return. They exchanged the dumpster, but he still came back.

The summer was coming to a close and the Fish and Game warden said that he would move on after we had left. We weren't worried. Bring him on, we thought. We have a foolproof escape system in place. He can eat the adults. But we will be fine on the lake shore. Basking in our engineering skills. The last week of camp, we were spooling down. There were no more hundreds of kids running around. No more scoutmasters or counselors running around. The season for outings was over at Camp Billy Rice. Our only access to the outer world was via radio phone in the main building. Thursday rolled around and the camp was silent. We had been feeding only the staff for the last three days. It was beautiful. The sky was crystal clear and the kitchen was hospital clean.

We retired to the cabin for one of the last nights at the camp. I was awoken by what started as a scratch on the door, but quickly escalated. I had lost one of my roomies as his parents came and picked him up. That left three. How much could a bear eat? I had to be the first to get away to safety. But I was in the top bunk, farthest away from the window. The scratches on the door were relentless, but subdued. That bear was setting us up for the big dinner. Then it all happened in a blur. The infantile screams that came out of that room that night weren't mine. Ok, maybe a few of them were. The next thing I remember is the rear window sliding open. The scratching intensified. We went into full panic mode. Before I could react, they had kicked out the screen. We all had our own pulleys. Yup. We had dug up some pulleys from that outbuilding and we all had our own high-speed, untested, well-lubricated pulleys. On a quarter-inch cable tightened to the twang of a guitar. I heard only a few things in the following seconds. Screams were in there. Splashes were in there. And STOP, it was only a chipmunk.

Those most important words saved me from what I found out was quite the experience. They hooked their pulleys on, and started down the cable. The scream came not from fear, but from the amazing speed they had accumulated in such a short time. Ok, maybe fear. Because neither could reach the ground to slow themselves, they continued accelerating, at a brisk pace, towards the lake. By the time they had reached the end of the cable, fate took over. I envision the carnage over and over. Actually, I envision them both going end over end in continuous revolutions till they reach the relative safety of the lake. Not really on the edge. About 20 feet out in about 10 feet of water. I will repeat that these are crystal clear waters from the snow-covered mountains into this natural lake. Some say cold. I say refreshing. I unhooked my pulley and stood back. The counselors were running to the lake, but I knew everything was ok. They were screaming in two different tones. As they came up the hill wrapped in blankets, they leered at me. It seems the three musketeers became two that night.

    I felt bad but continued to giggle and snort just imagining them flying helplessly, end over end into that brisk mountain water. I slept well that night. With one eye open.

WALKING THE OWNER

All Schipperke owners know that the dogs aren't controlled by the owners. They have the ability to Schippertize the owners/snack carriers into a false sense of security. By doing so, they create a situation that most can relate to. Loose Schipperke syndrome.

Now, I have had my adventures with this difficult and perplexing syndrome. As evidenced by some of my stories. But, I still aspire to be the best owner/snack carrier I can be. So, I take my two little black dogs for walks, in public, occasionally. It's not that I don't enjoy being dragged down the greenbelt at insane speeds.

It's not that I don't love the attention they get when they actually slow down and enjoy all the people that line up to give them hugs and scratches. But I learned this last summer that there was a way to control our little black dogs. No, not with shock collars or collars that constrict their ability to breath and therefore live.

The first thing you must do is find a collar that wraps around the chest and behind the front legs. They must be snug. Schipperkes have ruff. And a very thick coat. The first time I put a harness on Coach, he slipped right out. Thank goodness he was just as shocked by the freedom as I was. In that instant, he froze. And I swooped in with the finesse of a lineman reaching for a loose ball. I decided it wasn't in my best interest that the collar was loose enough to step out of, even if it meant I compromised good looks. I cinched that puppy down. It made it through that layer of fluff and into the body. The first thing he did was to turn on the reverse lights, trying to step back out of the harness. Awe. I was hurt. He couldn't get out. Luci was sitting there watching us both, snuggly in her collar. And not wanting to face my wrath. One of the few times you will see a Schipperke sit still.

As we proceeded down the greenbelt, I came to the realization that they were scheming something. Things were going way too well. They were not bothered by the bikers whizzing by at warp speed. Or the pit bulls that seem to be so prevalent in our area lately. Funny. Those pit bulls were held in check, mostly by marathon-running ladies that would outdistance and mock anyone that dared to encroach into their personal space. Pit bulls. I will stay off my soapbox after this little disclaimer. Pit bulls are unpredictable and dangerous. Enough said. Bet I'll get some love letters for that.

As we proceeded down the greenbelt, I looked and saw Luci was suddenly interested in the right. As we drifted into the grass, she swung left. Over Coach's lead and into oncoming walkers and runners and bikers. I pulled her towards the right and Coach headed left into the oncoming walkers and runners and bikers.

We have a delineated, clearly marked set of lines on our greenbelt. They are multicultural and painted on the cement. But they are not in dog language. My two dogs had decided that it was so great to see the guy on the other end of the leash panic. So, they started the little crossover game. After piling up a few runners and wrapping up some walkers, it was in my best interest to find another way. Out into the parks I went.

We have parks bordering most of the Boise River. So, when the kids get rowdy and decide they have minds of their own, we detour into wide open spaces. Soccer fields, softball fields, disc golf all over the place. And I detour to the local Zamzows to get a different lead. Then we have the S-word. That furry, long-tailed little rodent that taunts my Schipperpups daily in the summer months. I can't mention the S-word in my house for fear that my blinds will be torn from their mountings. That may have to do with my soft heart. My Ss don't have a peanut field in our neighborhood. In fact, I believe the closest peanut field is a thousand miles or better from my home. So, to keep the Ss from starving, I supplemented their life with peanuts. No salt. It created quite the stir in the neighborhood when the other Ss found out the chow line started at my front porch. I also felt it was necessary to give them water, so I kicked the birds off the bird bath and made it a S-bath. I seriously thought about filtered water with a fall, but stopped short with city water.

Fresh. Each day. On my front porch. Well.

During the days, I kept the blinds up a little so my kids could survey the hood and bark the necessary alarms if intruders came. I rearranged the front porch with a patio table and threw some bird seed out there to compliment the S-action that was going on. But, I made a mistake. I sat that table at the end of my covered patio at the front of the house. With bird food and peanuts on it. The dogs had enjoyed the interaction having the Ss running around on the ground. But, when they came eye to eye with them, the game changed. I was lying on the sofa on a Saturday morning. It was bliss. The dogs were by my side. The TV was showing reruns of Laurel and Hardy. And the blinds tilted so that we could survey the hood. Now, I don't know what set off the chain of events. And, to this day, I still don't know. But, an S said something to another S and all heck broke loose.

I looked up and saw two Ss rolling around in a flurry of fur, peanuts, and bird seed. The dogs went nuclear. They hit the windows in two short jumps and hit about halfway up. And they grabbed on to the blinds. Down the window they slid. With the curtains following, mounts included. The sound didn't faze them. Back into the windows they went. The Ss were rolling into the windowsill and it was tails and teeth. The dogs were blinds and teeth. As I jumped up, I saw a blur fly by the window. And one of the Ss disappeared. The other one was lying on the table looking around. We were all wondering what had just happened. The S froze. The dogs went silent. And I opened the door.

As I opened the screen door to survey the damage, I looked down and a hawk was wrestling with the S. And it wasn't winning. It was a little hawk and I don't think it knew what it had gotten itself into. The S broke loose and headed, full S-speed right past me, over the table, clearing it by miles. Across the yard, and to the relative safety of the tree. Squirrel one, hawk zero. Oh. I said the squirrel word. Dogs one, blinds zero. I once again digress, to my walk.

We merrily strolled across the park with no other dogs or humans in close proximity. Darn, I just said squirrel, didn't I? The dogs suddenly froze mid-stride. Now, this newfangled lead I got is amazing. It's elastic. And it's a Y. My hand holds a fishing reel where I can spool out up to 25 feet, to give them some free run. But they have to do it together. And this makes for some very entertaining times when one wants to go in one direction opposite to the other. This Y lead connects them to each other and then it hooks to my fishing reel lead, where I have some drag to work with before they reach the limit. I can slow them down gradually and lock it up if they are doing bad things. Like barking.

But, this day was going to be my challenge day. Schipperkes can't pull like a Husky. And they know their limits. For the most part. But they have surprise on their side. And lightning-fast zoomie speed. For those of you that bought this book, just because it had an amazing angel on the front, prepare to be educated. Schipperkes are able to attain the speed of a small corporate jet when they are given the proper stimulation. And that stimulation is rabbits, rats, mice, birds, and SQUIRRELS. Yes, I said it again. Thank goodness the kids are sleeping next to me. Because they know the sound of a computer typing squirrel. There, not 30 feet from me, on the ground, in the open, appeared a squirrel. He appeared to be alone, but I knew they ran in vicious packs. Selectively taunting all that threatened their domain. And I couldn't see his co-conspirators anywhere. But I was wary.

Luci and Coach were distracted by the scent of the last 300 dogs that had watered the bush they were next to. It's as if they were reading the Washington Post version of pee on the bush. Every twig had a different story. And there were highlights they had to read. They didn't see him. They didn't hear him. And he was in the strategic position of being downwind, so they didn't smell him. I made noises. I kicked the rocks around. I tried. But that squirrel just stood there. Frozen. Was he trying to push my buttons or just scared stiff? I knew better. It was game on. The dogs had managed to thread themselves into the bush, so I started the process of untangling one at a time. I got Coach loose, and went in for Luci. Then, eye contact was made. The Schipperke VS the squirrel.

I looked up and saw Coach on point. Ears up. Eyes glued to his target. And every muscle of his 20 pounds slowly adjusting to mount the attack. I normally carry snacks in a plastic bag. These snacks serve to break the concentration of a Schip when they are starting to go the wrong way down a one-way road. Trouble-wise. When the dinner bell rings, they generally turn for a token glance at the potential snack. Even they can be fooled. Occasionally. Well, I was in a hurry. Bad day to leave the prime rib at home. As I ducked into the bush, I felt a tug on the lead. Coach was primed and ready. Luci was in the bush. I was pulling on the Y lead to get her loose. Coach was acting like a winch. Each inch he moved forward, she came out a little more. Please try to realize, this all happened within maybe fifteen seconds. I'm just trying to slow it down for you Schipperke beginners.

As Luci came out of the bush, Coach felt the immediate pressure release on his lead. Luci was just happy to be loose and as she jumped up to thank me, Coach had his moment. Coach outweighs Luci by almost twice the weight. Give or take a couple of pounds. But it's enough that when he wants to go in a direction, we both have to at least listen. He took off like a flash. Given his size, Coach can still attain pretty impressive speeds in a short amount of time. Even with Luci and me in tow. See, I laid down the fishing reel to get Luci out of the bushes. Now, there goes the fishing reel bouncing down the walkway. Luci is an innocent victim at this time. She has no idea why she's getting dragged down the sidewalk, on her side, in a direction opposite of where her human is. But Schipperkes are quick to recover from situations and up she popped onto her paws. Coach was in full speed mode and she saw why. A frozen squirrel. Not cold frozen. Just terrified frozen.

The fishing reel was dragging behind. I was talking in a foreign language, which is my normal panicked thing to do. There was no way I was going to catch two Schipperkes, by myself, in the park, with them chasing a squirrel. The squirrel seemed to flick his tail in a taunting sort of way, till they got about 5 feet away. Two Schipperkes, on point, after a squirrel, normally means Schipperkes one, squirrel zero. Today marked a moment in history that the tables were turned. The squirrel took off towards the tree with the Schips after him at full speed. For the most part. Luci is by far the fastest Schipperke I have owned. And her body lends itself to speed. Coach not so much. Coach is like the train. It takes time to build up speed. But once he gets going, it's game on. The squirrel was just inches ahead and I envisioned the headlines in the news the following morning. TWO SCHIPPERKES SHREAD ONE POOR LONE SQUIRREL IN AN OUTMATCHED FIGHT IN THE PARK IN DAYLIGHT. Kids traumatized for life.

I was on my best run, given my age, to the inevitable accident scene when the squirrel made a quick left turn. It was just enough. Coach slid into the corner and Luci went to the outside. Not by her choice, but by gravity's choice. The squirrel hit the tree at just a little under the speed of sound, followed by Coach dragging the recovering Luci. This was my saving grace.

That day, the Y lead proved its use for those of us that have flight risks for dogs. They hit that tree trunk and proceeded to create the biggest mess I have ever seen. Coach went up the tree. Luci was still in full afterburner trying to catch up. She blew right past the trunk and then was redirected, by the Y lead, back around the trunk. Coach was coming down the tree from his futile attempt to join the squirrel in the branches. And they both ended up in a big tangled mess at the bottom.

Each day, I reflect on how long it would have taken two Schipperkes, on a Y lead, to find some immoveable object that they wanted to go to each side of. My chances in the park were greatly increased by the massive number of trees with squirrels in them. I don't hold such a death-grip on that fishing reel lead anymore. And I try to go to parks with a lot of poles, trees, park benches, barbecues, etc. If they get away, I'll get the phone out and record the train wreck that will ensue. The squirrel won that day. But we will be back. With our Y lead.

SHE JUST RAN OUT THE DOOR

We have all experienced it. I was a Route Manager for an industrial gas and equipment company here in the valley.

Each day, I would load my compressed gas cylinders onto my flatbed truck and head out into the mayhem of the valley traffic. I considered myself a courteous driver with a clean violation record in the truck. After work, I wreaked havoc on the valley in my personal truck. Paybacks to the people that made my stress level jump to just shy of my head exploding levels. It was spring and my other half got off and, upon arriving at the house, turned the air conditioning on. Now, it's only 75 degrees outside, but she is in a corporate office with AC that will freeze the nuts off a squirrel. I have to move from the relative comfort of the cab into the outside air at each stop.

So, I was acclimatized to the outside temperatures. AC was a luxury. And it seemed that my AC worked so well in the winter. And my heat was awesome in the summer. I think the mechanics reversed the switches just to save fuel. But I couldn't prove it. I was resigned to opening the windows to heat the cab in the winter and keep them open to cool it down in the summer. My other half called and asked if I had pulled the cord to the AC. I said I couldn't do that as it was wired directly into the breaker panel. Although that had my thoughts stirring on how to put a cord on it for future situations. She complained that the house just wasn't cooling down. I interpreted that as, "I can't get ice cubes to develop in the toilet." So, me not wanting her to get sweaty, I called the AC doctor and pleaded for prompt service. As it just so happened, they had a tech in the area and he would go right over. I called the other half and told her to open the garage door and allow him to go through the house via the kitchen door. She said ok and the conversation ended at that.

As I was headed back to the shop, I got a call on my personal cell. I don't answer my cell while driving, keeping up with my courteous and responsible semi-driver attitude. Then it rang again. I ignored it. I was only a few miles from the shop, so I ignored it. Then it rang again. Ok. I'm at a stop light. I'll check the voicemail. It was my other half. And she was screaming something I couldn't understand. So, I called back. She answered and was crying and screaming and saying some rather bad words. I told her to calm down and asked what had happened.

"Did he give you the bill and we would have to refinance the house to pay it?" Sasha had gotten out.

As I came into the shop lot, I rolled into the back and hit the air brakes. The truck slid to a stop. I was on the ground before it stopped. I ran through the shop and threw my paperwork on the desk. I told the receptionist that my dog was loose. And before anyone could say a word, the shop was silent. And I was gone. As

I zigzagged through traffic with the skill of a NASCAR driver, I asked, in a rather loud voice, "What the hell happened?"

There were a few other words thrown in, but I can't say them. I could tell she was really upset and it came to a time for calmer heads to prevail. Call the police. Call the fire department. Call the FBI and the CIA. Hell, call out the National Guard. My heart was in my throat. And I was in full-blown panic mode. She said that the tech had come through the garage door, into the house. And after checking the thermostat, he went through the sliding glass door, into the backyard. He came back in and said the fan motor was bad. Note: This AC unit is only two years old, just out of warranty. He said he needed to run down the road to get the motor. When he came back, he took it upon himself to take the shortcut. See, I have an access door that goes directly from the garage to the backyard. But, being a Schipperke owner, I have it locked. I also have two additional latches. And I have stacked up so much crap in front of it, that in the event of a fire, I would be found halfway through the pile, clinging to a plastic sawhorse, deceased. But, somehow, this tech decided to clean it up and move everything away from the door. He unlocked and opened the door and my guess is that Sasha was through that opening in milliseconds. By the time he shut the door and told my better half, she was gone. I live in a one way in, one way out neighborhood. And I love my neighbors. We keep an eye on each other and help when we can. Most of the time, without even being asked.

But, at the end of our little world, is a two-lane road that has thousands of cars run down it every day. The few times the Schipperkes got loose, I was able to corral them into the subdivision. And by the time they had gotten around the block, they were ready to go lie down and rest. As I rolled down the main street, I was looking in every direction for a black streak. Nothing. I drove around all the neighborhoods around me with the windows open, yelling "SASHA!", till I went hoarse. I started crying. And trying to get out "SASHA!" as best as I could.

Each person I saw, I stopped and asked if they had seen a little black dog. Each said this way and that way. I followed all leads. I envisioned driving down the main street and seeing her broken dead body in the middle of the street. She wasn't streetwise. All she knew is full speed, head down at every scent. She had no idea what a car would do to her. And I cried. I drove in gradually widening circles from the house, yelling "SASHA!" every 50 feet. Every dog was SASHA. Every shadow was SASHA. I cried. It got dark to the point that trying to see a little black dog was impossible. Maybe someone had taken her to the Humane Society.

Each night, they park a truck outside of our Humane Society for the public to drop off strays. So, I went up there that night. No Sasha. The next morning, I drove around the neighborhood looking for that body on the side of the road. I knew there was no way she could survive running around all of these big city streets without being hit. Before I went to work, I went by the Humane Society and checked the cages. No Sasha. I cried. I got to work and received token sympathy from my co-workers. "It's only a dog. Why are you so upset?"

I said, "It may be just a dog to you, but she is my fur kid to me." My eyes were welling up with tears. The manager said we still have customers to take care of, so I loaded my cylinders and freight, and took off. I broke records that day, finishing my route in super-quick time. And maybe broke a few speed limits, too. Then I spent the final few hours of the day driving around my area, in this big semi, leaving my business card to everyone I saw. And a message on the back: "Please help bring my Sasha home."

That night, I drove in ever-increasing circles outward. I checked the Humane Society and left my phone number and name just in case she showed up. I spent each day doing the same. And each evening driving around the streets around my neighborhood.

My other half had pretty much given up after four days. But I was out there each day driving and each evening driving. But after six days, even I was starting to lose faith. I was despondent, depressed, and hoarse from yelling Sasha's name so many times. The other half had moved on. I refused to give in. Or to give up. My baby was out there somewhere. It's amazing how such an event can turn one's life inside out. And I found out a lot about our relationship in those days. And how cruel people can be when they just don't care about dogs. "Get over it and move on." "She's gone." "Get another one."

Like that would do anything to close this raw wound that had festered into a debilitating disease. I wasn't going to stop till I had closure. I wasn't going to give up on my fur kid. That Sunday, at church, I went and asked for divine intervention. Our church, after services, asks all those that have special requests, to come forward. And they have prayer groups that will come pray over you. That day, I knelt before God, and I prayed. I cried. And as I knelt there, my pastor came to me. Our congregation is huge. And I was just another sheep in the flock. But that day, as I knelt before God, I had a special connection with my pastor. He had heard about my fur kid and held a huddle with a bunch of the prayer group. That day, I found out there are a lot of people in my church that love dogs. And I wasn't alone. I stopped counting at ten that were headed in my direction. And they laid their hands on me. I felt the love of God that day. And I felt the love of my congregation.

I went to the Humane Society truck that night and there was nothing. The next day, I started what had become a routine with me. I was to the only one left who believed that my fur kid was still alive. I got up, drove around my neighborhood yelling Sasha's name over and over again. I went to the Humane Society and checked the cages. And I went to work. I stopped updating everyone on my lost dog status, because they didn't care anymore. Everyone was over it, except me. I loaded the truck and planned my route around driving around my neighborhood with my big loud semi. Again. As I was driving back into the shop at the end of the day, my phone rang. I was driving, so I let it go to voicemail. It rang again and I sent it to voicemail. I pulled into the shop and back into the loading dock and the phone rang again. What? I answered and it was the other half. Our conversations about my obsession about Sasha had gotten more and more heated, so I didn't really care to hear from her about something like the washer isn't washing or the dryer isn't drying.

My family had given up on Sasha. I hadn't. She said the neighbor had come by the house and said she saw a little black dog behind the insurance agency down the street. She scared it when she was mowing her yard, but shut the mower off when she saw the dog. My other half was on the way to see if it was Sasha. I ran through the shop and threw my paperwork onto my desk. Before anyone could protest, I was out the door and burning rubber out of the parking lot. I might have caused a few close calls that day. But as I raced home, I prayed that it was Sasha. I came sliding down the street, jumped out of the truck, and ran inside. As I swung the door open, I looked over on the couch.

There was my SASHA. My baby. My fur kid. I ran over and grabbed her and held her gently, and kissed her face and head. I started crying. I took her back to the bathroom and gave her a bath. I cleaned all the mud off her as I cried. And I gently held her and dried her off. And cried. I slept on the sofa that night with only her next to me. She laid down and rolled in close to me. I put my arms around her and held her close. We slept. Peacefully.

The tech was buried in the backyard, next to the cable guy. Just kidding.

THE END

Thank You

There are many people that made this book possible. Through the Kickstarter campaign, personal donations, and through sharing and encouragement via social media. Thank you from the very bottom of my heart.

Amy Curran	Arlien Kennedy
Gabby Maria	Helen Rixon

Alexandra Bezuyen

Aleysha Clark

Amy Burkemper & Spanky Lee

Amy McDonald

Andreas Kaluza

Barb Barton, Bear, Havoc and Mayhem

Barbara Kelley

Barbara McClew

Barbara Murray

Beth Grant

Bruce and Melinda Money

Camilla Hansson

Carol L. Burnett

Carole Reesink

Carolyn J Price

Catherine Norwich

Cathi Theiss in memory of Skipper

Cherrie Rasmussen

Cindy Zellmer

Codey Lechtenberg

Cynthia Atkins Brandl

Dalene

Dave Tatro

Dear Brad and Julie - thanks for loving our breed! Xoxo from Hans, Bukka, Lilly, Jake and LuLu

Deb, another crazy Schipp mom

Deb King

Deborah and Helen Gallo-Eliadis

Debra Mascaro

Debra O'Leary
Del & Leisl Shagen
Denise Robinett In memory of all my schippies past and present
Donna Keihl
Dorothy Clem / Doreve Schipperkes
Dr. Jazzamae Pudderson
Frankie Hong
FSF Thistle Weed & AmyJ Harrington
Gale Sammons Welch
Gator, River & Booker Finch
Heather C. F. Case, DVM
Heather Smith
In memory of Grizzie and Love from Kodi McGee
In memory of Sasha, Gizmo, and my mom Florence.
J Saunderson & Luci Fur
Jackie Bennett
Jake Waffles Abney
Jazzy Enderle
Jean J. Miller
Jennifer Nicklyn
John & DeeDee Genaw
John & Lolly Espy
Joy Jensen & Al Franzone
Julia Maus, Malinoid-Schipperke
Julie Thornburg, Petagree Grooming
Karen Loth & Douglas Smith
Karen Rae Litt
Katherine Arlien Kennedy
Kathleen M LaGreca

Kyle Kincaid
Laura Nettleton
Lea Murray
Leah Ann Bergeron Jones
Lori Bertrand
Luann B
Lynn Hartke
Lynn Yaklyvich
Maggie, Taz, & Melinda Sipek
Marie-Françoise CAMPION
Mary Pilcher
Maureen and Dale Lobb
Melissa Lamont-Gordon
Micki Anderson
Myra Fonda
Nat, Pam and the Twittles' family
Norma Pacheco
Pamela J. Speigel
Paula C Loya
Peg Gross, Roadrunner Schipperkes
Rochelle Manderson - Adorin Schipperkes
Rowdy Fess
Ryan West
Ryan West
Sailor
Scout Stuart
Sharon Agresta-Siekerman
Shelli McCaskill
Sheradin Schipperkes

Smokey and Rosie's Mom
Steven Wright
Sue Waller
Susan Yoder
Tammy Stine
Tanya and Dave Dunning - In loving memory of Dakota
Tara Ollis- Mother of Schipperkes
Teresa Haertel
The Merrow Family
The Penny Smythe Family
Tita Kretz
Tonya and Rob Brown
Tulang Schipperkes
Val Smith Letham
Vicki Maher
Wendy Berry Pullin
Willow Vaughan
Yves, Dani & Skippy :-)
Zandra Zieman-Foster

122 | SCHIPPERTAINMENT

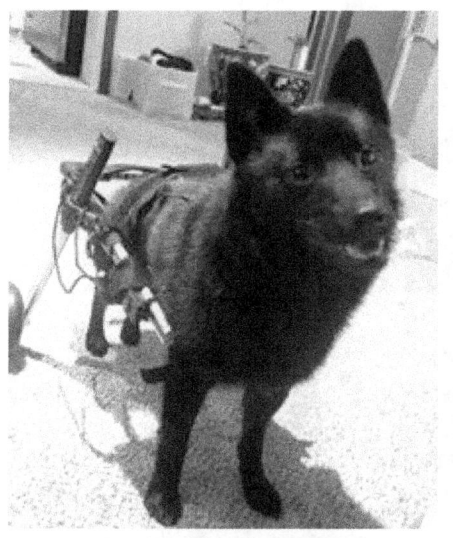

ABOUT THE AUTHOR

Richard Davis lives in the United States of America, in Boise, Idaho. He is a retired Air Force Veteran, and proudly served his time with Distinction.

'Schippertainment: Life as a Schipperke Owner' is Richards first published book, and came to fruition after much encouragement from the Schipperke Community worldwide. His stories were first shared on the Facebook Group 'Schipperke Country' and quickly gained a devoted fan base.

ABOUT THE ILLUSTRATOR

Amy Curran is an Australian Artist who graduated from the London Art College with a Distinction in Book Illustration. As a former Graphic Designer, Amy also enjoys Book layout and design.

When not at the computer, Amy spends her time with her husband and four children on their property near the Blue Mountains area of New South Wales.

Amy enjoys breeding and showing their Australian Cattle Dogs under their prefix Table Rock, and was especially drawn to producing this book for Richard about the relationship he has with his own dogs.

www.amycurranillustrator.com

Photo credit: Fiona Erskine, Ffire Photography

www.ingramcontent.com/pod-product-compliance
Lightning Source LLC
Chambersburg PA
CBHW062243300426
44110CB00034B/1672